Back When Kids Were Kids

Ron Albert

**A carefree era in the 1940's of a childhood gone by,
so let us take a walk down memory lane together.**

ISBN: 1500233757
ISBN-13: 9781500233754
Library of Congress Control Number: 2014911149
CreateSpace Independent Publishing Platform
North Charleston, South Carolina

DEDICATION

I dedicate this book to the "Sunshine" of my life, my wife, Darlene. She is not only the love of my life but also the inspiration in my life who has been the never-ending driving force throughout our life's journey together. She is always by my side. She was the one who brought me to the realization that I needed to continue with my note writing and create this book. Then she went one step further and said I should have it published for everyone to read.

My wife also edited each and every page, spending countless hours to help me form my notes into what you are about to read. Her continuing encouragement was for me to continue writing. Her efforts are a real testimonial to her commitment that each and every page be the best that it could be. Also, the front and back cover design concepts are her creation and should not go without recognition.

Also, I want to say thank you, in so many ways, to my parents Paul and Mae Albert for giving me the life that this book is about. I have mentioned numerous times throughout the pages what they did and how they loved me. In saying that, I want to acknowledge that their love, guidance and parenthood have not been forgotten.

I also dedicate this book for the edification of our wonderful children and grandchildren: Debi, Kris, Jen, Eric, Candice, Josh, Logan, Breanna and Autumn.

ACKNOWLEDGEMENT

Thanks to a friend, Don Miller of Distinctive Consulting, for his invaluable help.

Thank you, also, to those who have read and critiqued my book.

TABLE OF CONTENTS

Grasshoppers
Seed Pods
Playtime in Good Weather
Rainy Day Indoor Activities
Lead Soldiers
Metal Trucks and Farm Set
Board Games, Card Games and No Babysitter
Marbles

Chicken Coop
Catching Box Turtles
Sandbox
A Wanderer with his Wagon

Night Crawlers and Earthworms
My Favorite Fishing Place
Fishing with My Dad
Fishing Meant Quiet Time

Picnics at Home
Picnic Table
Horseshoes
Tree House
Tire Swing And Teeter-Totter
Bikes We Used
Ice Cream Treats
Candy and Gum
Long Walk Exploring a New Area
Blacktop Road

MEMORIES AS SEEN THROUGH MY EYES

I have often over recent years thought about jotting down memories of my early childhood. I now feel the need to do just that and will in the following pages try to put some of those memories down on paper before they can't be remembered. I want to reflect on them with you, the reader, as we share those moments together. Growing up and early childhood is a vast amount of who we become in later life. Those years in anyone's life have a distinct effect both positive and negative on our adult life. Take a journey with me back in time to a carefree childhood, in any town, U.S.A.

These writings are not a novel of fiction but real life experiences as seen through my eyes. Also, as you read about my early years you might take the time to reminisce about your own personal life and your own memories of days gone by. Remember, reflections are good for your soul and we all need to ponder that time gone by in this fast-moving world we now face each day.

Perhaps you will even want to share my stories or your own with your children. Whether the younger generation is young or old, we need to return to the family unit with love and compassion for each other guided by the "faith of our fathers."

With that in mind, let me start my recollections. I can only hope you enjoy reading these stories as much as I enjoyed writing them. The following may be from time to time just bits and pieces, and all the names may not be here. But the story is true.

MY ADOPTION

I was born in late 1940, somewhere in Northern Illinois. According to what I found out some years later, the time frame for being given up for adoption was sometime between the day I was born and two years later when I was adopted. I was in a Lutheran adoption home located in Addison, Illinois.

Paul and Mae Albert, who lived in McHenry, Illinois, legally adopted me. They corrected my birth certificate, which was recorded in McHenry County. I did find out many years later my true given name but never wanted to really go any further on that matter.

Through the years I have prayed for peace for my birth mother but just couldn't go any further out of respect to my adopted parents. They were all I needed and provided a very good existence. I hope and pray to this day that my birth mother is at peace with what had happened in her life to have to give me up for adoption.

To this day I can honestly say that my parents were loving, caring people. They were my parents, plain and simple. They raised me to be who I am today. They never pushed me nor did they want me to pursue anything that I was not comfortable in doing. I know that they both were very proud of me and loved me.

MY PARENTS' MARRIAGE

My parents were married on October 14, 1933. They were childless until I was adopted by them in 1942. I was their only child and to this day I can say I never was spoiled. I was pampered but only to the extent that I was loved and they knew how to raise me the proper way and in a good fashion. I was a very happy boy in so many ways and probably never demanded excess in any area.

I know they both were very proud of me throughout the years as I was growing up. In those early days children didn't demand or put unreasonable requests on their parents. Parents and my elders were always to be respected.

Marriage of Paul and Mae Albert October 14, 1933

MY DAD

My dad was somewhat strict but only as any father would be for his only son. His stern look was all I needed to realize I was in the wrong over something. I don't ever remembering him spanking or hitting me at any time. Words from him were always enough. We did and enjoyed so many things together over the years. I was his 'Butch.' I'm sure that he was very proud of me and even when I didn't follow in his footsteps as a newspaper printer, he was always proud of what I could do.

My dad worked for the McHenry Plaindealer, which was the local newspaper in McHenry for many years. It was a weekly paper typical of all the papers in the area. He worked there until we moved away.

We will share some more about my dad later in this writing.

McHenry Plaindealer Newspaper (dad on right and two others)

MY MOM

My mom was a kind and very gentle woman who never spoke a bad word to or about anyone. She had a sweet, peaceful soul and faith that she instilled in my life. She took such good care of my dad and me. She was happy in her life and doing for her family was all she ever wanted. She certainly didn't want for herself. She was frugal and carefully decided what was necessary to be purchased. She saved, reused and remade. It was another way to stretch the income. Her life lessons certainly came from the way her parents raised her. There again as I write my notes you can envision, as always was the case, that my mom was always there for me and did a fulfilling job on my overall development.

Beyond teaching me to say please and thank you was the fact that my mom herself always sent out short notes, thank you cards and letters. It was a normal, common practice used by most everyone in those days. My mom would also send letters to distant friends and relatives. No occasion was ever missed.

My mom would comment that a note of one kind or another needed to be sent and it was time to sit down right away. This was especially the case when I was told to write a thank you card for a gift given to me. No delay was tolerated.

OUR HOME IN MCHENRY

My parents lived at the time on River Road in McHenry, Illinois in a well kept home which sat on Fox River frontage. My dad had always owned a boat and outboard motor so the location with a boathouse suited them perfectly. I was told sometime later that shortly after I came to them, I was found to be throwing my toys over the fence into the river. Well, the story goes that shortly after that episode the house and property were sold and we moved.

I don't remember my dad continuing to own the boat after that time.

That move and relocation ended up being only three blocks away and only one block from the river. I'm sure it was due to the fact that they loved the area and perhaps the new house now suited their needs better. The property was about an acre in size with lots of room for a large garden and an oversized, detached garage with a workroom. The house was a Cape Cod style with a finished second floor bedroom that became entirely mine.

McHenry was growing at the same time I was growing up. The total population in the 1940's was probably less than 2,000. Homes started to be built in subdivisions and along each side of the river. Summer cottages that were already built were being remodeled and updated to all year round homes. The property along the river was starting to change in value. Since it was a town next to the Fox River, it had growth in regard to marinas, boat building and restoration. It offered all of the water recreation available on the river but it also connected to The Chain O' Lakes.

THE NEIGHBORHOOD

The neighborhoods in McHenry could be termed middle class with a blend of older homes and styles. All of the homes were well maintained. They were neither fancy nor out of the ordinary. Yards were mowed, usually with a hand mower, and kept neatly trimmed. Everyone took pride in the ownership of their home. Everyone knew everyone and there was always a greeting extended whenever meeting someone. Even the children and pets could be named at a glance. As a boy I could say hello to an adult but it was always "Mr." or "Mrs." whenever you spoke to them. That respect went hand in hand with "please" and "thank you."

Our home was always well maintained both inside and outside. The lawn was hand mowed and I was taught at a young age how to trim. I was given a hand held clippers that looked like large scissors. It was made of spring steel and one blade overlapped the other. With that design I had to squeeze the handle and then the blades moved over each other and cut. Always on my knees or bending over, it was quite a job for a small boy like myself.

PLAYMATES

In our neighborhood there were probably six kids or so who formed a group friendship. We would play together all year round at various times. Some of this I will mention later.

I also had a continuing friendship with Lonnie and Patsy, who only came out from Chicago on the weekends. I'm sure it was a real treat for them as it was for me to have them as playmates. The three of us would play for hours.

MY PLAYMATE CAROL

One of my constant playmates was a girl named Carol. She was about my age when she fell sick. At the time the rest of us would ride our bikes by her house day after day and wonder if she was well enough to play. That went on for some time and finally one day her grandfather said she was in the hospital. Later I found out that she had died. I was crushed. I had no idea of the magnitude of what had happened. I still was too young to understand but realized she just wasn't coming home.

MY DOG RIPPY

For many years I had as my constant companion a small, white terrier that I called Rippy. One time it seems that Rippy and I decided to take a walk and my mother had not been informed. It was just a little walk that must have taken us away from home for awhile. The story goes that my mother started calling and asking neighbors if I had been seen. No one said yes but one neighbor stated that she knew of an open pit or cistern with water in it that was nearby. Well, that sent my mother right over the top. Anyway, as the adults were preparing a search, I was seen coming across the old gravel pit with my dog at my side. Neither of us had a care in the world. I won't tell what happened next but you can rest on the fact that deep inside, my mother was extremely relieved. My special dog and constant companion, Rippy, was sixteen years old when she went on to doggie heaven.

MY RELATIVES

MY GRANDMOTHER

Let me take a few moments to reflect on my grandmother. Whenever she came visiting, she always wore a beautiful dress and carried herself like a queen. She was all decked out in jewelry and all the accessories. She had snow white hair and there never was a hair out of place. I still don't know how she did it, as the cars in those days didn't have air conditioning and it was a long ride out from Chicago with the car windows open.

When grandmother got out of my aunt and uncle's car, all of my cousins and I would immediately head for her. The reason beyond seeing her again was that she always had brand new, shiny quarters to pass out. We would stand in a semicircle and she would hug each one of us first. Then she passed out those prized, shiny quarters to each of us. I found out eventually that she went to the bank to get brand new quarters for us kids before each visit. One per person but you would have thought we had been given a bag full of money. Wow, a quarter in those days meant ice cream or a popsicle, for sure!

AUNT PEARL AND UNCLE WALTER

Aunt Pearl was my mother's only sister. My mother was quite short but her sister was much taller, probably six feet tall. When they stood together, they didn't look anything alike. Aunt Pearl always worked, so a trip to the country was a real treat for her. She and Uncle Walter always lived in rental housing so they didn't have a house, a yard or flowers. Grandma, who lived with Aunt Pearl and Uncle Walter, would all arrive at our house late Sunday morning.

Aunt Pearl would greet everyone in the front yard and then shortly after that she would be found walking through the house to the kitchen. She stopped only long enough there to pick up a salt shaker and then proceeded directly to the rear of the house and the vegetable garden. The next sight of her was seeing her walking up and down the rows, stopping frequently to pick or pull out a vegetable. Then standing there with one hand on the salt shaker and the other hand with perhaps a tomato she would put it in her mouth. After she had walked the entire garden and sampled all the vegetables, she would join the rest of the family for the picnic or the social time of the day.

Uncle Walter was a traveling salesman around Chicago-land. If I remember correctly, he sold industrial staples or something that pertained to production in factories. He drove many miles each day for his job. He may have worked on a commission basis of some sort, as they didn't have much money.

Uncle Walter's favorite car was a Studebaker. At that time Studebakers were made by Willys Jeep. Willys Jeep was the mainstay of the military vehicles in the war and very dependable. The story goes you could fix them with chewing gum and wire and they still would run. He would boast about how many miles he would put on each one. It was usually 160,000 miles plus. They were always sedans, dark in color and very plain.

One thought that has always reminded me of Uncle Walter was that he played the piano with no sheet music to call upon. Whenever there was a family gathering at my Uncle Wal and Aunt Meale's house, he would be called upon to play. Some prodding was needed and perhaps a fresh beer but then he sat down and began playing a non-stop segment of all types of tunes. I remember one time my two cousins Al, Wally and I were making too much noise and Uncle Walter stopped playing until we settled down. Boy, did we get some looks from everyone that afternoon.

AUNT AMELIA AND UNCLE WAL WITH THEIR TWO SONS, AL AND WALLY

Uncle Wal was my mom's older brother. They lived in Chicago on the Northwest Side on Austin Avenue near Milwaukee Avenue. I remember my aunt as being Italian with a rather large family. I especially remember her as being a great cook. Oh, could she prepare a spread! We always were served a large, Italian meal at her house. The one thing that stands out is she would insist that all of us boys should finish our meal so that it would make for a good day tomorrow. Those were her famous words. She gave great hugs and always had a smile for each one of us. Uncle Wal worked in a bank near Lakeshore Drive so he commuted by bus each day.

One time Uncle Wal got us boys tickets to go to Soldier's Field just south of the Chicago Loop. At that time there were stock or midget car races around the outside of the athletic field. Well, let me tell you, I was one excited boy as I had never been on the L-train or ever in a big arena like Soldier's Field. The day finally came and we all took off on the elevated train. I recall sitting rather close to the oval track as my uncle had gotten good seats close up. We were still in the concrete bleachers but close enough and just the roar of the cars going around that track was overwhelming to our ears. When we got back to their house, my aunt would say that even though it was late, we all needed to wash our faces and hands as we all were black with the soot from the track. Lots more memories later in this writing of my experiences with my two cousins, especially with Al, my younger cousin.

AUNT DOROTHY AND UNCLE ED

Aunt Dorothy and Uncle Ed had two daughters, Dorrie and Glee. We would see them from time to time at family gatherings. I don't remember them too well because we didn't see them very often. My aunt and uncle were both quiet and gentle people who just faded into a group setting. One little thing about Dorrie, my younger cousin, was that when we all shared a large holiday meal, all they could get her to eat was black olives. Can you imagine that, just olives? Uncle Eddie, my mom's brother, died at a rather early age from a heart attack so I'm sure it was difficult for my aunt to support herself and her daughters. Life insurance and company benefits were not the same then as they can be today. I don't know if Uncle Eddie even had life insurance. My aunt and her daughters just seemed to fade from the family from that time on.

UNCLE BEN AND AUNT HARRIET

Uncle Ben was my dad's only brother. He and Aunt Harriet had two children. They lived in Crystal Lake and my uncle worked for many years in the local hardware store. That probably was due to the fact that my great-grandfather owned a hardware store in Chicago on Belmont Avenue for many years. Perhaps Uncle Ben decided to stay in that type of business also.

UNCLE WALTER AND AUNT ELSA

Uncle Walter and Aunt Elsa weren't really my relatives but I was taught to call them by those proper names as they were good friends of my mom and dad. In those days you were taught to honor your elders in all cases. Those teachings went hand in hand with "please" and "thank you."

We would go to visit them from time to time at their summer home in Island Lake and at their home in northwest Chicago. One thing that stands out is that my uncle picked fresh mushrooms at their summer home. He would go through a cow pasture across the road from their house. By the time he got done and headed back, his pail was full of huge, fresh mushrooms. No one ever worried about eating them as he always knew which ones were not poisonous. Cleaned up, sliced and sautéed in butter, now that's an "Oh, boy!"

MY MOM AND DAD

MY DAD, A PRINTER

My father was a printer all of his life, working for the local paper. He knew and conversed with a lot of the townspeople, mainly from the newspaper and his church.

McHenry at that time was no different than any other small community. Everyone knew everyone. My dad made up for his shortness in height by how he carried himself. Even though he was short, he made up for it with his hearty handshake and how he greeted a person. When he entered a room, everyone knew him and respected him.

CHURCH BUILDING FUND

An interesting thought comes to mind about something my dad was involved in at our church. Our church was growing in members so the congregation started a building fund to buy property and build a new building. The funding was going rather slowly so my dad decided to talk to the priest of the local Catholic church. That church had a large congregation and a most distinct voice in what happened in McHenry. The priest said to my dad that he should place containers around town in the local businesses. He said to put a label on the outside of the container with just the words, "Contributions for a local church building fund. You really don't have to name the church unless you want the name on there. In that way you will get everyone to contribute. That's all you need to do and it will work." From time to time the money was gathered and those donations made quite a difference in the church building fund. The property was bought and the building went up thanks to the priest and his suggestions. In those days people were perhaps more understanding and all wanted to do their part.

MOM'S CHURCH MEETING

Another thought that I would like to share is what happened when my mom went to a church meeting in the evening. My dad and I would drop her off at church and then my dad would backtrack to his favorite tavern for just one glass of beer. The tavern was also a local meeting place for the town's residents. I would be allowed to come inside and get a soda and perhaps some popcorn or pretzels. Both of those items were always on the bar for all to share. At that point I could sit on the tall bar stool while waiting for my drink. Then I would get off the stool and go outside. I entertained myself by catching an assortment of nighttime flying bugs that were attracted to the neon lights. I remember one called a sand fly with a very delicate body and wings. Dragonflies were similar. All I did was catch them, study them and let them go. After an hour or so my dad and I would pick up mom and head home.

THE JUKEBOX AT THE TAVERN

The tavern had a jukebox that played selected records. It was a stand-up unit and about the size of a home refrigerator. It had all types of luminous glass with lighting behind. The lights would blink as the music played. There was a turntable with a playing arm with the needle attached. After the selection was made by pressing the keyboard with the matching number on the flip menu board, the fascinating part started. I could watch the arm reach out and pick up the right record, twist, turn and then gently lay that one record on the turntable. Another arm would then reach out and set the needle on the record. I always wanted someone to make anther selection because then I could watch the operation one more time. The jukebox became a part of Americana we all would see for many years to come.

DAD, THE NEGOTIATOR

My dad was quite a shopper for items from groceries to cars. For instance, he had no problem going into a meat market or deli and asking the butcher to cut off a sample of a lunch meat for a taste. Then he would ask for another slice from a different lunch meat. After tasting several, if not more, he would make his final selection and ask to have some wrapped up. The same would be true of the cheese area. I often thought that if he had been given two slices of bread, he had more than enough free samples for a sandwich. He also would pick out a wrapped piece of meat, walk over to the butcher and state that he wanted only a selected portion of that package. The butcher would then have to take the wrapping off and cut off that selected portion for my dad.

Whatever he bought over the years he was always a hard sell. I'm sure some of the regular salespeople he got to know saw him coming and knew that the sale would not be easy by any means. When talking about comparison shopping, he was the best! He knew his prices beforehand and exactly what he wanted to spend. For example, when he bought a car, it was a process of going from dealer to dealer to find the right deal. I was his buddy so I always tagged along and spent many evenings in car dealerships.

There was no one else who could do it better than my dad. I learned even at an early age how to negotiate on an item. It just seemed natural to him. I think it was also a sport to him. He never gave the salesman the idea he really liked one car or another. My mom would not be involved in that selection process. He never wanted to give the salesman the edge. Pricing was discussed and then my dad would say, "I'll think about it" or "the dealer I saw last week gave me a better price on the same identical car with the same accessories." Then the stand off would begin. My father would state that he could never figure out why certain accessories came in groups and groups only. If he wanted a light in the trunk and not in the glove compartment, he would say so. His theory was that the total group was too much money so he wanted it separated. When the salesman threw in the cost of the entire group for nothing, then he was happy.

If he had a problem with a car, for example, his solution was to go beyond the dealer and contact the manufacturer. It worked time and time again as most companies don't want a buyer to be unhappy.

DAD'S TOOLS

Even as a young boy I worked alongside my dad on all types of projects around our home and in his large workshop. I may have just sat by ready to hand him the next tool that he requested as I got hands-on experience to learn how to use a hammer, a screwdriver or a saw. My dad would say from time to time, "There's a right way and a wrong way to use even the most simple thing like a tool." Even with my being left-handed, he taught me the correct way. He would say, "Let the handsaw do the work, you just guide it and with a little, light push it will cut by itself." He also said, "The hammer is not a club so use your wrist to bring it down, don't beat it to death." I can go on and on about each tool but I learned the correct way to use each and every tool.

When we finished a project or at the end of the work session, I was shown how to clean and properly put that tool away. If we didn't anticipate using a saw, the blades were checked for sharpness and then rubbed down with a light coat of oil.

The same was true for garden tools. They were brought back to the garage and cleaned up before being stored. That meant scraping off all the dirt so nothing was left dirty. My dad would say, "It's easier to dig with a clean shovel then one that has dried dirt on it." There again if that tool wasn't needed for perhaps the rest of the season, it was cleaned, oiled and hung on a rack. I learned how to sharpen tools so those same tools were never put away dull.

The whole idea he gave me with his words of wisdom would best be summed up by these words, "Treat a tool or machine right and it will last for years." That is very true to this day as a lot of those same tools are still being used by me. I have his snow blower, which runs like a top and I use it every winter. With just an oil change and some grease, any quality tool or machine will last for years. My dad taught me that whether it's a piece of equipment, a tool, a car or whatever, these were major investments and should be treated properly to last for years.

My dad not only taught me how to use tools but due to his knowledge he taught me how to build, repair and do maintenance on everything we owned. He came from an era where so many people needed to be versed in a variety of fields. The reason was quite simple, money! He learned from his father and I learned from him. My dad needed to have the know-how because he couldn't afford to hire someone to do that same job. I couldn't even begin to describe what he and I accomplished over the years.

My dad may have been short in stature but he made up for that in so many ways. He was always someone to be reckoned with on so many subjects.

MOM

My mom didn't work when I was growing up. I'm sure my dad and mom decided that as long as I was home that that was best. She took excellent care of our home, my dad and myself.

The interior of our home was neat, orderly and most of all clean at all times. All of the furniture was in good condition and kept that way. Nothing was replaced until it wore out. When anyone came through the front door, they immediately felt comfortable and at home. Visitors would remark on that very fact.

MOM'S BAKING

One of the greatest joys I can remember is coming home as a young boy and taking in the smells that would radiate throughout the entire house from the kitchen. The smell of fresh bread, a cake, a pie, cookies or brownies would make any boy agree with me that the aroma made me hungry. How can one ever duplicate that smell unless it is from a freshly baked item? All I know from firsthand experience is that I reaped the rewards over and over of those delicious, home baked goodies. It was all thanks to my mom's hard work and her desire to do and give the best to her family.

Nowadays bread comes precut in a bag and desserts come in a box or are purchased already made. Stores today have even installed fans to draw the smells from their bakery area into the store so that it entices the customer into buying.

MOM'S RECIPES

Mom had a vast array of recipes that she used and collected over many years. Her mainstay in recipes were the "My Better Homes and Gardens" and "Chicago Daily News" cookbooks. The inscription in the "Chicago Daily News" book was:

"Dec. 25, 1935,"
"To: Mrs. Santa Claus
From: Mr. Santa Claus"

Mom regularly cut out recipes from the newspaper or magazines. They were kept in a kitchen cabinet and now are in my kitchen cabinet. The exchanging of recipes was also done between the ladies who perhaps were part of her craft circles.

MOM AND DAD'S GARDEN

I remember my dad having someone plow up the huge garden area. Then after the disking was done, all the hand work would begin. I learned how to dig and rake quite quickly. It meant not only raking the garden smooth but also making the rows, forming melon hills, and planting the potatoes and tomatoes. A long handled hoe was used to make the individual rows for the planting of the vegetables and seeds. All in all, it was a very busy time for all of us to do that planting. The fruits of that labor were renewed when the garden was harvested. A certain pride goes along with what each one of us had done to be a part of the produce in that garden.

MOM'S SEWING MACHINE

My mom had a "Singer" sewing machine in its own cabinet. The actual machine would drop into the cabinet by means of a disappearing shelf that closed the top over it. It had foot pedals and a series of rubber belts that drove the needle mechanism. By pumping the pedals faster or slower, you could adjust the speed of the needle. That sewing machine turned out numerous dresses, aprons, curtains, etc. At that time a lot of the women sewed because it was too expensive to go to the local store and buy the finished products. The local 5 and 10 cent store sold all the makings including fabrics of all types, textures, designs, needles, thread and any other notions needed for sewing. The full-size paper patterns were available in the store. There also was exchanging of patterns between the ladies.

No matter what my mom wanted to sew, it took quite awhile to mark, cut out and prepare the individual components before running the pieces through the sewing machine. My mom kept containers of buttons and various hooks that had been cut off a discarded piece of clothing before it was thrown away. When planning a new project, she always first checked that stock to see if she had the right buttons or needed to go to the store to buy new.

I can remember that mom wore on a daily basis, house dresses with an apron over it. The apron was worn all day and it protected the dress. If someone came to the door, she could quickly take it off to look presentable. She made all of her own aprons as my aunts and neighbors did also. Those aprons were made in two styles. One had a full front with a tie around the waist and the other was to be pulled over the head. Those aprons were just not available in the store except in patterns. I remember mom not only using cotton or denim yard goods but also taking apart flour/seed sacks. They were made of a heavier weight of cotton cloth. There was an appropriate amount of fabric from those sacks which was just enough to make a half apron with ties. The flour/seed sacks came in all sorts of floral designs and were too good to just throw away. Every item was used at least once if not more.

MOM'S ATTIRE

On Sunday or when going out, mom always had at least one good but simple dress. It was store bought so it was treasured. She wore simple jewelry, a watch and a good pair of comfortable shoes. At that time all the ladies wore hats and gloves whenever they went out. She didn't have a large wardrobe by any means. It consisted of perhaps one item for each special occasion. Each item was treasured and kept clean in her closet.

I would like to add that she never wanted much in the way of material things. She always was very happy to just take care of her family. That was her goal and she achieved it countless times throughout her lifetime.

MOM'S WASHING MACHINE

I remember my mom always used a wringer washing machine. I don't know when automated washing machines were invented but we never had one at our house. My mom preferred her wringer washing machine. There again it was her way of washing and she didn't want to switch. Only after my folks retired did my mom give in and let my dad buy her an automatic washer and dryer. The wringer machine had a huge tub for the water, a motor, an agitator for the actual washing and two wringers mounted on a post over the tub. The agitator would turn back and forth in a continuous action. Then the wash was rinsed through the wringer into the sink nearby and then back into clear water for a final rinse. The laundry was once again put through the wringers and then hung up to dry. It was quite a process to wash one load of laundry. Multiply that time by how many loads and it became a full day for her. All the actual drying was done outside unless the weather was bad or too cold. Then wet laundry was hung in the basement on multiple clothes lines. When hanging clothes outside, the first job was to string the clotheslines on hooks at prearranged intervals in the back yard. The rope was then gone over with a damp cloth to clean it. Then the wash was hung up and held in place by clothes pins. Support poles were often used under the lines to help carry the load of the damp, heavy laundry. A good drying day consisted of sun and gentle breezes. Then after the laundry was dry it was taken off the line, sorted and brought into the house.

I also remember that from time to time the temperature for hanging outside was marginal. Mom always wanted to hang the wash outside as it smelled so much fresher when brought inside. If the temperature was around freezing, the clothes would dry stiff as boards on the lines. They would have to be brought inside to thaw and dry.

What I just described regarding the washing applied to most households, not just ours. Mom did the laundry on Monday and the ironing on Tuesday. Ironing was a big portion of each work week as we didn't have permanent press material so each piece of clothing needed to be ironed. My grandmother was known to iron the bed sheets and pillow covers. All the men used cloth handkerchiefs that also were ironed. There weren't many items that didn't get ironed. Thus, it was an all day job for mom.

SAVING

RATIONING

We all were living in a time with the Second World War going on overseas so life at home was easy and simple. A vast majority of what we have now we didn't have then. It just wasn't available. So much went into the war effort. There was rationing of gasoline and of raw materials that were used for the war effort. I still have my dad's gas ration card which got stamped each time he used it for certain amounts of gas. That was all you got each fill-up. There were no long extended trips made during the war years. I'm sure a vast variety of other items such as food, clothing, sugar, butter, cigarettes, metal, and automobiles were unavailable. The simple things that we now take for granted.

SAVING

The dark red gas ration book, made of cardstock to fold like a wallet, held the coupon book, coupons and the inspection report

Gas Ration Book's Instructions

IMPORTANT INSTRUCTIONS

1. This ration can be used only for the purpose for which it was issued.

2. Within 5 days after discontinuance of the use for which this ration was issued, this folder and all unused coupons must be returned to your War Price and Rationing Board.

3. You must surrender this folder and all unused coupons to your War Price and Rationing Board before selling your vehicle. The purchaser will not be issued a gasoline ration unless he presents the receipt which you receive at the time of surrender.

4. All unused "T" coupons must be returned to your War Price and Rationing Board within 5 days after the expiration date shown on the coupon folder.

VIOLATORS of the Gasoline Rationing Regulations are subject to *revocation of rations and criminal prosecution* under the laws of the United States.

Gas Ration Book's Mileage Coupons

WE SAVED EVERYTHING

At that time in history a lot of what we used each day was not available or at a premium. Clothes, food and gas were just a few of those items.

Keep in mind that my parents and countless others had also just gone through the Great Depression prior to the war whether as children or as adults. They all had a different perspective on life and what it meant to have even a loaf of bread or the most fundamental items we now have at our immediate disposal. My mother saved all of the string that would be on a package. She folded up and reused the tissue paper, gift wrap paper and wax paper. Aluminum foil was not available as aluminum was used in the war effort extensively. My mother had a drawer in the kitchen that stored all those items, which were used over and over again. She continued that saving all the rest of her days. We just learned not to throw away items as they certainly could be used again. Socks were mended and not tossed away. When your shoes were starting to show wear, you took them to the shoemaker and he put new heels on them or perhaps even new soles. Nothing was discarded. It was all used again and again. Never forgetting that newspapers were also saved by all. They were tied up in bundles and gathered by organizations like the Boy Scouts at various times during the year. They actually would pick up the newspapers from your home or curb.

RECYCLING, REUSING

Old clothes were torn up for rags. Paint brushes were cleaned to be used over and over. Nails, screws, paper, string, bags, boxes and gift wrap were all saved. That was just a way of life in that era. Nothing went to waste.

POP BOTTLE REFUNDS

Collecting pop bottles was a good way to earn some extra money. Pop, beer and many liquids came in glass bottles. Pop bottles when returned to the grocery store were worth two cents each. I would always be on the lookout for discarded pop bottles. It we had some bottles at home, my dad would give them to me to return and I could keep the money. At best I could save enough for an ice cream so who could ask for more. My red "Radio Flyer" wagon was put to use for more than one purpose but if dad was driving to the grocery store, the bottles went along with him. That same wagon was used numerous times over the years for countless projects. By the way, it had been such a useful work cart for all of us that I still have that wagon today.

ALLOWANCE AND SAVINGS

I had a piggy bank for all of my money, which consisted of loose coins and small gifts of money like my grandmother would bring with her whenever she came to visit. I really never got an actual allowance from my folks. My dad firmly believed I might slack off from my assigned chores. He felt that I needed to earn it first. Then he and my mom would work out an arrangement as to how I could save enough money for a particular item that I might want to buy. From time to time I was given money for that small purchase at the store.

I actually had two small piggy banks. One bank was shaped like a barrel and the other looked like a bank vault. Both had keys that my parents kept in a separate, secret place. I would shake each bank and try to guess how much money had accumulated. Both my mom and dad helped me to understand the importance of saving. They also put aside money on their own to buy savings bonds for my future. Those bonds were purchased and placed in their lock box.

COMMUNICATION AND HOME ENTERTAIMENT

TELEPHONE

There was only one phone in most homes and that was located in the hallway of the main floor sitting on a small table, or hanging on the wall in the kitchen.

RADIO

Not every household was able to afford a TV so the radio was important to many people. TV broadcasting wasn't widespread until after the war. Everyone during that time would listen to the radio for their evening's entertainment and also listened intently for the news of the world.

Many people had relatives in the Second World War so that news touched almost everyone. Many of the famous radio stars later switched over to television in the late 1940's and 1950's.

THE FIRST TELEVISION IN THE NEIGHBORHOOD

I can't say when we all saw television for the first time but I do remember being asked over to the neighbor's house to see it for ourselves. The neighbor who had the unit worked for Zenith television and brought one home for his personal use. It was a stand-up model with a chest of drawers size cabinet. The screen was probably eight to ten inches wide in this large unit so we had to sit up fairly close to see anything. All of us sat in a semicircle and were entranced to be able to view such a new wonder. We were all just in awe to be able to see a cartoon or a special show like "The Lone Ranger":

> **"A fiery horse with the speed of light,**
> **a cloud of dust, and a hearty hi-ho, Silver!**
> **The Lone Ranger! With his faithful Indian companion, Tonto,**
> **The daring and resourceful masked rider of the plains**
> **Led the fight for law and order in the early West.**
> **Return with us now to those thrilling days of yesteryear...**
> **The Lone Ranger rides again."**

Or "Gene Autry":

> **"I'm back in the saddle again**
> **Out where a friend is a friend**
> **Where the longhorn cattle feed**
> **On the lowly jimsonweed**
> **Back in the saddle again...."**

Or "Hopalong Cassidy":

> **"Here he comes, here he comes**
> **There's the trumpets, there's the drums, here he comes.**
> **There he goes on his way,**
> **Down the trail the cowboy way.**
> **Hopalong Cassidy, Hopalong Cassidy..."**

Or "Roy Rogers," to name just a few:

> **"Happy trails to you, until we meet again.**
> **Happy trails to you, keep smilin' until then.**
> **Who cares about the clouds when we're together?**
> **Just sing a song and bring the sunny weather.**
> **Happy trails to you, 'till we meet again..."**

The picture would roll and be blurry but we didn't care. It was TV and we were seeing it for the first time sitting in that neighbor's living room.

OUR FIRST TELEVISION

When we did get a television, it was placed in the living room and never turned on during the day. Only when lunch time came could I sit in front of it to eat and rest. Then it was turned off and didn't get turned back on until my father sat down for the evening. There again it was his or mom's programs we watched and only their nightly programs. There were a few variety shows like "The Ed Sullivan Show," which I believe was one of the first evening shows aired on

37

Sunday. Part of his opening remarks were "we are going to have a really, really great show." Those few words would make him famous as a Master of Ceremony in the years to come. Another was "The Texaco Star Theatre" with Milton Berle as the host. His opening and ending segment had four men who came out on stage dressed in overalls and service station hats, and together they sang songs. The "Arthur Godfrey" show was a talent program. He had a segment of his own to play the ukulele and sing.

All of the new TV stars, whether they were comedians or singers, came from radio programs and prior to that from vaudeville. Radio started slipping in popularity so in order to keep their audiences they moved into television. One of the major breaks for them was the fact that their followers could now watch them on the television screen.

Very popular at that time were the westerns with a favorite cowboy actor in various programs of their own. The Lone Ranger and his sidekick Tonto, Roy Rogers and Dale Evans, and Gene Autry were popular stars on radio and then had their own shows on TV.

The stores then started to carry products associated with those TV programs. Toys, games, books, costumes and more were available for all the kids to buy. I had my share of those things as the western stars were my heroes. I wanted to be like them every day while growing up. Many a day I wore my cap gun in its holster on my belt. I also wore a pair of cowboy boots which, by the way, were not comfortable but they sure looked good! My friends and I would play cowboys and Indians for hours.

Author On Right In His Cowboy Outfit Standing In Front Of Chicken Coop With A Friend

Saturday was cartoon morning and some types of TV shows had a blend of puppets and other characters on the same show. One of those was the "Howdy Doody" Show. It featured a puppet named "Howdy Doody" and the emcee was Buffalo Bob. Many of us can still remember the opening theme song.

Buffalo Bob: "Say kids, what time is it?
Kids: It's Howdy Doody time!
It's Howdy Doody Time.
It's Howdy Doody Time.
Bob Smith and Howdy Do
Say Howdy Do to you.
Let's give a rousing cheer,
'cause Howdy Doody's here,
It's time to start the show,
So kids let's go!"

Buffalo Bob was dressed in western cowboy attire as well as his puppet. The show had an array of other characters that would have some part in each show.

Notice I said only one TV in the home. TV waves were transmitted from tall towers located in and around Chicago. Those radio waves were sent out to our own antenna, which was mounted on the roof. Every house in a neighborhood needed an antenna. They were rather unsightly, to say the least. There again the bigger and taller antenna you had would get you even more and better reception. Some even had a motor attached which would turn your antenna to get better reception. If you lived near a broadcasting tower you could get by using what they called "rabbit ears." There were two small arms with a small base that sat on the top of the TV. By pointing them towards a tower, you might get some better viewing. Of course, you had to move them from time to time to make sure they were pointed just right at one station. Channel change meant a rabbit ear change also. It had to be just right. Also, the local TV channels went off late at night and at that point all you got was one picture, which was called a test pattern. All the local channels were set up with that test pattern. They only broadcasted so many hours each per regulations. Early the next morning the channels started up again.

TO MY READERS –
LET'S TEST YOUR MEMORY

1. What TV commercial's jingle was "a little dab will do ya?"
2. What was the breakfast of champions?
3. Who had a basket of fruit on her head?

Answers to Test
1. Brylcream
2. Wheaties
3. Chiquita Banana

SPRING

FRONT SCREENED PORCH

There wasn't any air conditioning in any part of our house but it had a large screened porch that we all just adored. Lots of hours in the summer were spent there. Every evening many a meal was served out there. A metal framed and padded glider was the main piece of furniture along with several chairs, tables and lighting. We enjoyed the porch not only on clear evenings but also any time it rained, day or night. Just a great place to hang out!

The Author Sitting In Front Of The Screened Porch

EVENING SOUNDS

In the summer evenings we could sit out on the porch to read, talk or just listen to the nighttime sounds that only can be heard when it's quiet. Crickets were plentiful and made noise well into the evening after dark. We just never wanted to have one in the house because they never stopped making their sounds. Cicadas were also nighttime bugs making continuous sounds. They made their noise by rubbing their two hind feet together which was their way to call out to each other. Many sounds of nature can't be duplicated.

Lightning bugs, also known as fireflies, were always common. They are the little, flying bugs that come out in the early evening. The underside of their bodies glows with

43

a sort of greenish, luminescent color. I have since learned that that color change is part of their mating scheme. What great fun we had in trying to catch them in flight and then putting them in a glass jar to watch their bodies glow off and on. The jar always had to have a top on it so it could be punched with holes to give the lightning bugs air. Grass had to be added and always a stick or two for climbing.

GRASSHOPPERS

The same would be true for the grasshoppers that we would catch throughout the summer. Again we used a glass jar to capture these bugs. Trying to catch grasshoppers was great fun, as they jumped whenever we got near, so we ended up chasing them running and jumping like crazy. There also was a variety of grasshoppers that were called flying grasshoppers. They could actually fly for upwards of twenty feet or so. Now that's a real chase in a field as we never knew where they were going to land or in what direction.

Going out in the yard and trying to find a four-leaf clover was always a good way for one of the adults to keep all of my companions and me busy. I only found one that I can remember. I kept it for some years in my wallet.

SEED PODS

Another item that comes to mind are the seed pods that floated down from the maple trees in the spring. They looked like two small wings attached to an individual seed pod. As they floated down, they appeared to be actually spinning as they dropped to the ground. That is truly the case as those two wings helped to give the seed pod a gentle way to reach the earth. Of course, they covered the ground waiting to take root in the soil or grass. Most of the pods dried up but perhaps a few made it to the next step. Just another way that Mother Nature made sure that the trees continued their life cycle to produce again and again.

Another tree with a seed pod was from a catalpa tree. It had a long seed pod that looked like a bent cigar. My friends and I would collect them and place them on a table not knowing what to do with them. We had great fun just picking them up because they were so unusual. If we had planted all of the seed pods we probably would have ended up with a forest of trees. That was not the case. Even when discarded and thrown in a pile, they never took root. Keep in mind our Lord only gives us what we need, never too much of anything including new trees.

PLAYTIME IN GOOD WEATHER

Whenever the weather was good, we as kids were out-side all day from morning to evening. The only time we came in was for lunch and a rest afterwards. It could be on some-one's porch or even just resting in the shade outside but it was a rest time for sure. There was no TV watching during the day. We all were too busy to just sit and do nothing. I was prompted to read and to this day I am an avid reader.

Outdoor games were played. One game was hide-and-seek. One person was "it" and the others would run and hide. We tried to get back to home base without being tagged. When one of us would get back to the free base area, that person would yell out, "Ollie-Ollie-Olson Free" or "Here I come, ready or not, stick your head in a coffee pot." Then the person that was it went out again to search for someone else. We played baseball and kickball, tossed footballs around and jumped rope.

RAINY DAY INDOOR ACTIVITIES

On rainy or stormy days I was content to play by myself. I had enough simple toys, books and comic books to fill my day. If it was warm, I would sit on the front porch. If it was cold outside, I played in my room.

LEAD SOLDIERS

One of the toys I had was a set of lead soldiers. The figures were about three inches in height and very detailed complete with colors. When I think back now, I remember it was a set that my dad had from when he was a child. They were already old when I played with them. With that set I could set up battles right on my bedroom floor.

METAL TRUCKS AND FARM SET

I also had some metal trucks that I played with both inside and outside in the sandbox. Some were the size of my hand while others were much bigger. I didn't have many but enough to enjoy for hours at a time. When friends came over, they would play with them like they were brand new. I had one truck that I could actually sit on if I wanted to ride it. I didn't because it was too valuable to me and I didn't want it to break or have a wheel come off. I had a farm set complete with animals, fences and several buildings. The buildings were made of light, gauge metal while the animals were made of a plastic-type material that was available at the time. There again I would set up that complete farm and would just sit next to it and play farmer. Sometime later my dad bought some farm equipment that actually were miniature replicas of real equipment found on farms. I kept those in their original boxes because they were a real treasure. Later on I gave them to a cousin who played with them like I did for hours.

BOARD GAMES, CARD GAMES AND NO BABYSITTER

When inside there were board games such as "Monopoly" and all kinds of kid's card games like "Old Maid" and "Fish." A deck of playing cards was always close at hand so we could make up our own games. The adults would play cards for hours. Their games were canasta, pinochle, bridge and perhaps some poker for the men. My mom and dad would spend an entire evening playing cards at home or if they went to visit friends. I can remember going to someone's home and while the adults played cards, I was left in the living room with treats and pop to fend for myself the entire evening. My parents never hired a babysitter for me because I was always included in their social activities.

MARBLES

Marbles was another game we could play. All the boys at that time had a box or small bag of marbles not only to play with but also to trade. We, of course, had to have what was called the shooter marble. It was bigger than the rest and was used for just that purpose. A circle was drawn out about three feet in diameter and players would sit around the edges and shoot marbles. There was a certain way you flicked your thumb and that was the trick to shoot the large one in an effort to knock the smaller marbles out of the circle. Those became yours for the next game. There were several marble games that were played with various rules for each. I remember going to grade school one time with my marbles in hand to play in a tournament. Circles were drawn out on the gym floor with tape and teams were chosen. What great, simple fun could be had with a box full of marbles!

Whenever we looked at a marble up close, we could clearly see the different colors and ribbons of color in them that made no two alike. Each one was beautiful in its own right and when they were put in a tray the colors were outstanding. Little did we know at that time that they would become collector's items and worth a lot of money.

STORIES OF INTEREST

CHICKEN COOP

On the property that my folks owned was a used chicken coop. Lots of windows were across the front side with a service door and racks built on one long back wall. My dad decided to raise chickens. Before getting the birds he not only cleaned up the coop but prepped the racks with straw. He also cleaned up the run yard in front. It had a tall fence around three sides with no way out except back though the actual coop. All seemed to be ready for chickens so my dad proceeded to purchase some hens and, of course, he needed a rooster.

All seemed just right except for one thing. The run area didn't have a fenced top on it. You can guess what happened that first night. All of the chickens got out including the rooster. The problem was that no one told my dad that he needed to clip their wings so they couldn't fly. Well, fly they did, directly into the next door neighbor's trees. The neighbor was very upset and my folks were equally upset. It was a long night for my dad to take a ladder and retrieve each bird by their feet and haul them back into the chicken house. I'm sure they all wanted to just roost and sleep the night in the trees. Needless to say, they were not allowed out in the run area until fencing could be installed over the top and their wings clipped. I was sent to bed so I don't know how long it took my dad to retrieve them one by one. The relationship with that neighbor was never the same as he worked in Chicago and had to get up early each morning and didn't appreciate the rooster's wake up call. It was a very short night for all.

CATCHING BOX TURTLES

Not far from my house and the neighborhood was a swamp area that actually was only the backwater from the river. Lots of creatures lived there. One of them was the box turtle, which was common to that type of water setting. Every early spring the females would come out of the swamp and wander up to solid land to dig a hole and lay their eggs. After that was done the nest was covered. Then the females would wander back down the slope to the water. It was a rare find for us boys so we proceeded to go back home, gather some buckets and get back to the migration. Picking up the turtles was a bonanza but after filling several buckets and taking them home we discovered we had no use for them. Then after a parent realized what we had done we were told to march directly back to the swamp and return the turtles to where we had found them. Releasing them was not nearly as much fun as finding them. But, oh well, we sure had fun that day.

SANDBOX

In that same back yard was my sandbox. It was about four feet by eight feet in size and had two seats at either end at an angle in the corners. There again, like the picnic table, it was never moved due to the weight. My playmates and I would spend hours doing all the things children do with sand. Each year there was a given time when the red box elder bugs took over my sandbox and literally covered the sand. They liked sitting on the sand because the sand was warm. We didn't play in there for awhile. They normally just flew away eventually.

A WANDERER WITH HIS WAGON

There was a man who passed through town early in the summer. I remember going with my dad to the north end of town. There along the road in the ditch line was a man standing alongside his wagon and team of horses. He was a sight to see as if he had just stepped out of an old picture book. He was dressed in a very old pair of bib overalls, an old shirt and work boots. He had a long, gray beard and hair to match. His outfit was topped off with a wide brimmed hat. The team of horses consisted of two old, tired-looking horses and some goats were tied to his wagon.

The Wanderer
And His Wagon

He stopped on the side of the road to rest the team and sell some trinkets and postcards. There always was picture taking by the bystanders, my dad for one. I guess the wandering man came from somewhere south and was heading north. He probably was just a rambling soul who got great comfort out of his life on the road. More than likely he sold those trinkets in order to exist. Staying with his wagon and team, he was obviously living a very simple life, not causing any trouble but just meandering north. Then he probably headed back south in the fall to warmer climates.

He reminded me of the early settlers and their wagons complete with pots, pans and numerous other articles hanging from the side boards.

> "I love to go a-wandering,
> Along the mountain track,
> And as I go, I love to sing,
> My knapsack on my back....
> ....I wave my hat to all I meet,
> And they wave back to me...."

FISHING

NIGHT CRAWLERS AND EARTHWORMS

Before fishing at my favorite pier or going with my dad on a short fishing trip, it was always necessary to collect worms. For regular worms, all I had to do was go out to the back garden area. I would dig up the area where leaves, coffee grounds and some of the vegetable cutoffs and peelings had been left as mulch. The worms loved that mixture, which eventually made good compost to be used in the garden. The worms stayed under that damp mulch and survived quite nicely. Using my dad's pitch fork made it easy to uncover the worms. The trick was to dig them up right before I went fishing so that they didn't die. I was taught they needed to be alive so they would wiggle while on the fish hook. Then they were put into a discarded metal can to take with me when fishing.

Finding night crawlers was an entirely different search. My dad and one of my uncles taught me how to catch them at night. They told me the night crawlers only came out at night and could be found in our front or back yard. All we needed was a flashlight and a can. Then shine the flashlight on a certain, small area of the yard, locate one, bend down close to the crawler and grab it, being careful not to squeeze it too hard. Sometimes the crawler would pull back into its hole before I could even snatch it. If I did get hold of one, I didn't know which end was the head compared to the tail. Lots of times I would gently pull and the crawler would be heading back into the hole. I was told to "try, try again." If I was fortunate enough to get some night crawlers, they were the most desirable worms for fishing. Big fish needed to bite on big worms. It's that simple!

I recall how I was taught to put a worm on the hook. My dad told me to hook it in multiple spots, leaving both the head and tail loose so the worm would wiggle on the hook. Wiggle was the word!

MY FAVORITE FISHING PLACE

My favorite fishing spot was close to home. The location would almost always guarantee me some fish. There were boat slips and piers at a restaurant-bar called "Snug Harbor" on the Fox River. Pan fish called bluegills, crappies, large sunfish with bright, orange bellies, and perch were always to be found there. It was about three blocks from my house and two doors from our original home on the river. Note, it only took a number of years and I was back on the river. I would go there with my worms and a short pole. All I had to do was bait the hook and drop the line and bobber over the side of the pier, letting the bobber float under the pier into the cool shade. There were always pan fish resting in the coolness of the shade. The perfect spot! I would either sit on the pier or lie down so I could see the bobber moving. Customers using the boat slips had to go around me. I never totally blocked the walkway so I was never, that I can recall, told to leave. Perhaps I made such an impression that who could say anything to a young boy fishing.

Author Holding A String of Fish

Once I caught a very big rock bass with beautiful colors and markings. I was so excited that I ran home and was able to convince my mom that I had to keep it alive until my dad could see it when he got home from work. To this day I don't know how she allowed me to put it in the basement yet alone in a tub. I'm not sure if it was her laundry tub or just a large pan. At the time I was so excited I forgot that fish can jump. Well, it did and it died. I was crushed that my trophy fish was no longer of this world.

FISHING WITH MY DAD

In reflecting back, going with my dad on fishing excursions to the Chain O' Lakes, which was part of the Fox River waterway, were other joyful times. Other times we would be on vacation in Southern Wisconsin. Either way it was a special time, as any boy would agree. What a day it was for me to be out in a rowboat with a motor! We had all the gear and perhaps a snack lunch because we were going to catch some real fish. I don't ever remember any really big ones, just the usual pan fish. They filled our live net, which hung over the side of the boat. It was my job as I sat in the bow to pull the basket out anytime we moved the boat. Also, by sitting in the bow with my dad at the motor, we balanced out the boat. When we moved the boat, I still remained in the bow, this time turning around in my seat. I would then get splashed with the water spraying over the bow. It still was fun as I could sit up there, pointing to the water and feeling at that point I was the commander and seeing nothing in front of me but the water. It was always a delight to reach down into the water spray and change the direction of the waves with my hand.

My dad always liked to fish, either with a bobber or most of the time with the pole, no bobber and set over the gunwales so the line would go directly down into the water. He always tested the depth and made sure his hook and line never reached or dragged on the bottom. The bait was worms that we had dug up at home in our yard and garden. He would then hold onto the line with his fingers so he could immediately feel the fish nibbling on his bait. He would spend some time fishing just like that. I always wanted to use a bobber and toss my line out a ways from the boat. In my mind it was like there weren't any fish close enough to the boat. By doing that, you had to be doubly alert to the floating bobber. The slightest motion of that bobber could mean a fish nibbling or just the motion of the water. That rocking motion would almost put me to sleep the more intently I gazed at it.

I can also remember that when the fish were not biting, my dad would start calling them. His famous words were "ooggily–woogily." It was like the saying, "fishy, fishy in the brook, come and bite on my hook." That really never helped but it kept my attention level somewhat high for the next fish to bite. He had a fishing tackle box that was filled with lures, hooks, bobbers, sinker weights, extra line, etc. It was a treasure of items that had passed through the years safe in that box. I was given my own tackle box but never to the size and quality of my dad's. The only dreaded part of the trip was getting back to shore and cleaning the fish. All I can say is it was messy and smelly!

FISHING MEANT QUIET TIME

It was a requirement of my dad to remain quiet while fishing. His words were simply, "You'll scare away the fish," so if we wanted to talk to each other, it was in a very low tone.

SUMMER

PICNICS AT HOME

My family would have gatherings at our house because we had a good sized yard. Among those family members who came were Aunt Pearl; Uncle Walter; my grandmother; Aunt Meale, Uncle Wal and their two boys, Al and Wally; Aunt Dorothy, Uncle Edward with their two daughters, Glee and Dorrie. It wasn't very often that we could get together, as it was a long drive for all of them who came from the northwest portion of Chicago and River Grove. For them it meant driving two-lane highways all the way with every town in between.

Family Picnic At Our Picnic Table

PICNIC TABLE

In those days one always needed and used for various reasons a picnic table. My dad built one out of all two inch material including the top, all the supports, braces and support legs. The benches were also made of two inch framing. Needless to say, that table and those benches were so heavy that it would take four men to lift and move them. My uncles would all complain to my dad about the weight when it had to be moved into more shade. All the men would give a hearty laugh or two over the weight of the table while lifting it to the new location.

Everyone brought a dish to pass or a dessert, so we had plenty of food. There was always a lot of iced tea and homemade lemonade. There probably also was beer but since the men were the drivers, no one had too much to drink.

HORSESHOES

After the lunch was served, the men would gather under the shade trees to rest for a while then on to some pitching of horseshoes. My dad always had a horseshoe pit. I always wanted to be able to pitch but the weight of an actual horseshoe and the distance to the other stake was not possible for me. Forty feet was too long of a distance for a young, small boy. Just the sound of the shoes hitting either the iron stake or each other is a memory in itself. There is no other sound like metal hitting metal or men kidding and carrying on over a game of horseshoes.

TREE HOUSE

I remember that our property backed up to an old gravel pit not used any longer and all overgrown with brush and trees. Well, that was a playground like no other! It had hills and dales, overgrown trees, brush and weeds along the outer edge. It was a perfect spot for a playhouse under the overhanging branches of one large, old tree. Under that tree, we set up a complete playhouse with broken furniture, pots, pans and whatever else we could find. It provided shade and coolness from the summer heat. We had various rooms set up. No one ever had to worry about climbing up a tree or the possibility of falling. We just stayed under the limbs in the shade. Many hours were spent there just pretending.

TIRE SWING AND TEETER-TOTTER

In my neighborhood we had at least one good old-fashioned tire swing. That swing consisted of a long, stout rope tied from a strong, overhead tree branch and a worn-out car tire tied to it. That was all that was needed for hours of enjoyment. The only true swing sets were found at the grade school or at one of the city parks, both of which were too far to go just to swing.

Another item was a teeter-totter. One of the dads in the neighborhood would make one for us. All that was needed was a sturdy, strong sawhorse and a large, wooden plank. We didn't even need handles. All we had to do was hang on. We felt we were on a bucking horse. The more limber the plank was, the better the ride. Sometimes the other person would get off abruptly without saying anything. At that point if you were still on your end, there was only one way to go but down, hard! It was great fun until we felt somewhat dizzy from the up and down motion.

BIKES WE USED

I can't remember when I was given my first two wheel bike but from that moment on a new, broader world opened up. Now I could comb the neighborhood in a matter of minutes. Wow! Keep in mind that in those days we all knew the boundaries set up by our parents and there was no going beyond those points. From that day forward I lived on my bike or it was always close at hand.

My playmates and I wanted to pretend we had motorcycles so we installed a small playing card with a clothes pin on the frame of the back wheel. When the wheel went around, it hit the card and caused a constant clicking sound. It was all we needed to make our bikes sound different. The stiffness of the card determined the sound. Later on in my childhood I was given a basket for the front handlebars so I could carry all types of things. Of course, I had to have streamers attached to the handle bars, which consisted of bright strips of ribbon and rubber handles. Perhaps a headlight, a bell or horn would be needed and used.

ICE CREAM TREATS

In the summer it was always a treat no matter where we were to have ice cream. It could be with my folks on a Sunday drive, at parties of all kinds, at the carnival, at the ball park or wherever ice cream was available. It was always a special treat.

I remember specifically getting money from my mom and going to the small neighborhood store. It had a little bit of everything in the way of groceries, pop, a milk cooler, ice, bait and a gas pump. I can still remember the outside front of the shop. The thing I recollect the most was that inside the store was a small ice cream counter with three stools. Ice cream cones were ten cents per dip and a milkshake was twenty-five cents. The owner of the store also had a cooler stocked with popsicles, orange-flavored push-ups, fudgesicles, dreamsicles and ice cream cups sold with a small, wooden spoon.

My favorite was an ice cream sugar cone with two dips of my favorite flavor on top. The first dip was always straw-berry. Strawberry was my mom's favorite flavor and I'll tell you why in just a moment.

The shop was located about six blocks from my house, so I always started to eat my cone from the top. I always made sure I didn't get into the strawberry unless the ice cream was melting too fast. Of course, then I had to lick it also. I had to move rather quickly as the ice cream would melt in the heat. By the time I got close to home, I had worked my cone down to several inches from the bottom of the cone. The bottom dip was strawberry and when I got home, I always gave the last bites of cone and whatever ice cream was left to my mom. I can still see her standing there in her apron which she always wore and saying something like, "Yum, oh, yum." Boy, was I proud at that moment! She would then say what a special treat that was and gave me a big hug in addition to many smiles that moms are so good at giving.

CANDY AND GUM

Besides ice cream treats, the candies and chewing gums I recall were "Double Bubble" gum, jaw breakers and "Cracker Jack" popcorn that had a free prize inside the box. Some of the stores had gumball machines with small pieces of gum in a machine that only cost a few cents. Many of these same treats are still available today.

LONG WALK EXPLORING A NEW AREA

One sunny afternoon my friends Patsy, Lonnie and I decided to go another way along River Road to explore. We decided to get off the road and cut through a farm pasture. Mind you we didn't have a care in the world. Off we went across that pasture, crossing over the wooden fence with the barbed wired top. There were no problems until we came back out near the farm house. We all were surprised when we heard the lady of the house yelling, "Get out of that pasture this moment." We hot footed it out, only to find out from her that her bull was in that same pasture and obviously didn't like our company. Luckily for us we got off with a stern warning. We never did see the bull but that was alright as we really didn't want to meet up with it anyway.

BLACKTOP ROAD

On our long walk back home after the bull incident we were hot and tired. There was a little stream of water so we decided to cool off. We took off our shoes and socks, dipped our feet in the water and thought we might as well walk for awhile with our shoes off. Walking on the side of the road, which was all gravel, didn't feel good. So we decided to walk on the actual road, holding our shoes. It was hot on the pavement and the tar had melted just slightly. The bottoms of our feet were instantly covered with tar and dirt. Upon getting home, we were put to the painful job of removing the tar. We used plain soap and lots of water for scrubbing. We all knew that when my dad got home it would be turpentine, gasoline or some nasty paint brush cleaner and that would truly hurt, so we hurried in our attempt at removing the tar. Obviously, we never did that stunt again.

SWIMMING LESSONS

McHenry had at least one swimming park that was directly next to the Fox River. It had a sand beach among other things. That is where I took swimming lessons and consequently learned how to swim several of the basic strokes. I never liked diving, so I didn't pass that part of the training. The class had Red Cross certified instructors. At that time the river was clean enough for swimming. Now many years later we never would even think about swimming in the river. It's sad that the water is so polluted now.

4th OF JULY PARADE

McHenry always had a big parade on the 4th of July weekend. There were other parades throughout the year but none as big as this one. The saying that "everyone loves a parade" is so true and whether young or old everyone gathered for the parade.

There was a huge turnout along the entire route that passed through downtown. I can remember going with my folks and standing at the same location each year. There were numerous bands, color guards, lots of flags, and Armed Services floats, which consisted of the local veterans and their wives all sitting on a decorated float. Floats from every organization were part of the parade including marching bands, fire trucks, EMC's, water rescue boats on trailers, Boy and Girl Scouts to name but a few. I can also recall my dad taking 8 mm motion pictures with his camera. A grand time was always had by everyone that afternoon.

FIREWORKS

The 4th of July wouldn't be a special celebration without fireworks. There may have been a fireworks display somewhere in town but I don't remember. All I remember is my dad bought some small fireworks for our own viewing pleasure. He would set them off in the front yard. We never had large firecrackers, only small cones that when lit produced a display of multicolors. I also was given what were called snakes that would crawl across the sidewalk. Lady fingers were a very small firecracker about 1 ½" long and maybe ¼" in diameter and could be safely lit on a connecting string. Then it was one pop after another! There were always sparklers and when lit, I could run around and twirl them every which way in the darkness of late evening. I know that the bigger boys in the neighborhood had much larger firecrackers called cherry bombs and M-80's. Those were loud and dangerous.

Another item available in those days was the cap gun or pistol. The caps were small dots of gun powder which were connected on a long, continuous paper roll. When inserted into the gun, we had a cap gun that could fire numerous pops just by pulling the trigger over and over. If we didn't have a cap gun, we could always just find a sidewalk or hard surface, roll the caps out and fire each one by hitting them directly with a hammer.

CARNIVALS

McHenry had two carnivals each year. Both were held in the city park. If I'm not mistaken, one carnival was put on by the VFW and the other by the American Legion. Both were very large in my eyes, as both organizations were well supported in town.

I can remember going with my mom and dad. The thought that sticks in my mind is that when we got there, the first item of business was to locate the bingo tent. Once we found it, my dad would give mom some money and she would sit down and proceed to play bingo. At that time my dad and I would wander around the rest of the carnival and check it out. I never was much for rides like the Ferris wheel and the Tilt–A-Whirl. Those rides were too scary for me. There also were throwing games, ring toss, roulette wheels, and Pick the Duck, which always netted a prize. There were lots of lights and noise, foods of all types and, of course, cotton candy.

I just mentioned that there were certain carnival rides that I didn't enjoy and consequently didn't try. But there were a vast number of small individual booths that offered lots of different kinds of prizes. The prizes were on shelves along the back wall to catch our eye from a distance. Those prizes certainly caught my young eyes.

There were many different ways to win a Kewpie doll, a fancy hat or even a very cheap toy. There was a ring toss over pegs or bottles in the center of a booth set on a low platform. That game seemed easy enough even for a kid my size. The ring had to be held just right and tossed to land on the pegs or bottles. The tricky part was that the ring had to land just right on the peg or bottle to slide down enough to be counted as a win.

Throwing a baseball to try to knock down a weighted figure on the back shelf was another game of chance. Lots of times if the ball was not thrown hard enough, the figure would just wobble and not fall down.

I really wanted to try the game that tested one's strength but I was just too small in size. I couldn't even lift the mallet let alone swing it. Bigger boys or men were given a very large, heavy mallet with a head the size of a football to swing mightily to hit the pallet dead center. Then the connecting arm would fling a ball up a tall, fixed runway. Markings on the side indicated how strong the hit was. Prizes were given out according to those marks. It really was a true test of strength and could be an embarrassing moment for the men and boys who didn't do as well as they thought they could. So my dad and I just watched as others played the game.

Oh, the duck pick-up game was the easiest of all the games. People paid the cost, went over to the circulating tank and picked out from the water a little, floating duck. On the underside of the duck was a number that corresponded to a number displayed on the prizes. That game was too easy for me as it presented no challenge, so I opted to take a pass. I told my dad, "It's for little kids, not me."

Penny or quarter tosses into a bottle from a set distance was yet another game of chance. It was pure luck if a coin of any size would land inside that bottle. It seemed easy enough but all eyes were on the person playing. I felt that my money was safer in my pocket and decided not to play.

For adults there were roulette wheels. The person betting would pick out numbers and colors and place their coins on a corresponding number and color. Then the wheel was given a hearty spin and the player waited patiently for it to stop on their chosen number and color.

One fascinating event about the carnival was being able to go with my dad once to watch from a distance the actual set up of the units. Those units all arrived via trucks and trailers. When all the pieces were put together, it was quite a spectacle. Right before my eyes a complete carnival was unfolding. There was always a group that traveled with the carnival and they were called carnies. They appeared to be a rough looking group of people, who lived in campers and basically stayed by themselves. I was told by my dad that I should stay away from them.

Later on my dad and I would wander back to where mom was sitting and she always surprised us with her winnings. She always won at bingo whether it was a blanket, a Thermos bottle, a picnic basket or a kitchen gadget. Some of those items I inherited and they were with me for many years to come. They had great prizes in those years. I know that some if not all of the prizes were donated by the local businesses.

BOAT RACES

In midsummer there also were hydroplane boat races starting at the same park I mentioned above and continuing south for some distance. The river was blocked off at either end for safety. There were several rather large marinas that supported the races. Hydroplane boats were very small, flat bottom boats powered by very large outboard engines. Those high-powered motors towered over the boat and driver. The boats seemed to just skip over the water and flutter like a little bug. They easily could turn over as they just rode on the top of the water and did not draw much draft as they moved. I'm sure we watched the races from our neighborhood beach as they turned around right in front of us. During those turns was when the boats seemed to dance the most. I can still hear the constant, high-pitched drone of the engines as the races ran off and on all afternoon.

WEED CUTTING MACHINE

Speaking of the river, another thought comes to mind. It is not of great significance but fascinating to me as a boy. There was a weed cutting boat that would go along the shoreline on either side of the river. This flat bottom boat looked like a barge with a big comb on the front. The cutting bar was located there and was equally as wide. A conveyor belt would carry the cut weeds to the back to be unloaded later on shore.

Even with all the boat traffic, weeds were a problem and had to be dealt with each summer. The weeds could make great mulch if you wanted to spread the weeds in your garden. As boys we were very impressed at how the machine worked and we would sit and watch it go by very slowly.

SUMMERTIME CARDBOARD SLEDDING

In the summer we would try to find a piece of cardboard to use for sliding down a hill. It sometimes worked if the grass was long and just a little damp. If no cardboard could be found, we would just lie down on our side and roll or tumble down, rolling over and over. We became quite dizzy and from time to time looked really silly trying to stand up right away as we swayed from side to side. It was yet another way we entertained ourselves without any manu-factured or purchased items. It's interesting that by using our imagination we were able to entertain ourselves with just a plain piece of cardboard.

THE SWAMP CLOSE TO HOME

As I mentioned before in regard to collecting turtles at the swamp, it was a drawing card for me to walk along the edge of the swamp and check it out from one end to the other. It had to be checked out every so often in case some-thing changed or a new creature would be discovered.

Another attraction to my group of neighborhood friends was the fact that we wanted to build a raft. We didn't worry about going out in the actual river as the only waterway to it was through inlets which weren't big enough for the in-tended raft. The swamp wasn't that deep out in the center so we were safe from harm. Most little boys have a dream about building a raft. Well, we decided to make that dream a reality. The process started by all of us was to go out to search for the necessary materials. We searched the neighborhood and came up with bits and pieces of building supplies. As I recollect, the raft wasn't very big when it was finished and it didn't really float very well either. When two of us were on the raft, we stood in water over our ankles as the raft slipped below the water line. That was OK because we all had been part of living out a dream.

When walking along that swamp I found myself looking for tadpoles (very young, tiny frogs) and for adult frogs. Trying to catch a frog was another matter. Like grasshoppers, they could sense my presence and immediately would either leap into deeper water or hide under the cover of the weeds and grasses. Then I would have to start all over.

Tadpoles in the early spring were easy to find. I took a cup, a bowl or a piece of screening to catch them. I didn't want to keep them so I took a quick look and released them. I also tried to catch some minnows but released them quickly so they could grow to be bigger fish. Both tadpoles and minnows were easy to see because the water was clear enough for me to see their motion from several feet away. Even at my early age I was beginning a catch and release program of my own.

THE PASTURE THAT SURROUNDED THE SWAMP

Our small neighborhood was next to an open cow pasture, which was bordered by the swamp. That field was used by the farmer so the cows would be in there every so often. The cows never bothered anyone. It was the bull we had to watch out for whenever we crossed to the swamp.

Sometimes when we walked through the pasture, we played a game of chicken. The idea was to see if we could step between one cow pie and another. If we did, we got an instant surprise on our feet. We carried our shoes just in case. We didn't do that very many times before learning it wasn't worth it. From then on we walked between the cow pies trying not to step on any of them.

BARBED WIRE FENCES

I learned at an early age that there was a right and a wrong way to cross through or over barbed wire fences. There were several fields in the immediate area like the one that needed to be crossed to get to the swamp. We could have gone down the road but it was out of the way. If I was by myself, I would always crawl under the wire on my stomach. If someone happened to be with me, we would take turns stepping on the bottom wire and holding the upper wire with our hand. That created enough room for us to bend over and crawl through. We never tried to climb a post and go over the top. Barbed wire points are very sharp and I learned quickly how to negotiate a fence.

ELKHORN, WISCONSIN COUNTY FAIR

Each year my parents took me to the Elkhorn County Fair located in Elkhorn, Wisconsin. It was in late summer. It was a sight to behold as there were acres and acres of fairgrounds. The fair was nothing like anything I had ever seen before. I was able to see up close livestock of all varieties, namely cows, steers, pigs and horses. There were also chickens, ducks, geese, rabbits and other fowl. All the animals and the birds were housed in huge barns.

Farm equipment of every make, style and color was available to look at. Small equipment, feeders, pens, fencing, water troughs, hand equipment, lawn mowers and wagons were spread out in a large, open area. I could actually climb up on a tractor, sit down on the seat and pretend for several moments that I was really driving it. The moment was so exciting for me!

The 4-H was well known and represented by a lot of the various clubs who were participating in the fair. It was a unique experience for young people who had an animal at the fair. They could actually stay with their animal in sleeping areas set aside in each barn. By doing that, they could not only feed, wash and brush their animals accordingly but could be a source of comfort to their animal. Each type of animal was reviewed by a group of judges who then awarded ribbons in various categories to the animal's owner.

The fair had numerous sheds and buildings that housed 4-H items in groupings of vegetables, flowers, canning, homemade bakery goods, quilts and art work. Several buildings housed businesses displaying their products for sale.

The midway consisted of all the rides and small booths with assorted games and prizes. They were basically the same variety that I saw at the carnivals. Even though we would walk along the pathways, I never seemed to have any interest in them. My mom never played bingo at the fair because it was too big and out of her league.

In the afternoon there were horse races called sulky races. The term came from the fact that the horse was strapped to a small, two-wheeled pull cart. The driver sat very close to the back of the horse. If the horse turned suddenly, so did the cart. We would sit in the grandstands and high enough to be able to see the entire track.

Before each race the driver would parade his horse and sulky in front of the grandstand. At that point everyone could see each horse and driver up close. Then mom, dad and I would make our personal selection of a winner and as the race began, we kept track of our choice for winner. Then the people in the stands, along with us, cheered on our favorites. There was no money involved, no betting, just some wholesome family fun! Of course, my dad would be cheering the loudest but no one cared since everyone around us was also rooting for their favorites to win.

After the races were over, it was time to head home. We were all weary but realized it had been a great afternoon.

THE LAST DAYS OF SUMMER

Our garden had everything growing in it: potatoes, to-matoes, various types of lettuce, green beans, onions and carrots. There were also several types of beans, peas, cabbage and melons. Most of the vegetables were started from seeds, which were saved from the previous year.

CANNING

Canning was just something folks did, especially if they had a big garden. All those vegetables needed to be dealt with in their own harvest time. Potatoes were dug up and stored in gunny sacks. Carrots and onions were dug up. They all were placed in sacks or bushel baskets and put in a cool, dark place like the basement.

My mom did a lot of canning and preserving of the bounty from that garden. Not everything was bought at the store in those days. This was true not only during war time but how families were raised. Grow and can the garden produce to enjoy in the wintertime. In the fall it was a great task for my mother to do that job. The problem with canning was that when a particular item was ready to be harvested, she had only a matter of days to harvest and preserve it.

I can still remember the large, dark blue, enamelware canning pots and kettles that were needed not only to cook the vegetables but also one for the sterilizing of the jars and lids. Each type of vegetable needed to be put up in jars with lids and rubber-type seals. It took countless hours for mom in that hot kitchen. I can still remember sitting in the living room after a canning session as my mom kept track of how many lids popped. We all would keep count and say out loud, "There's another one." If it didn't seal and pop, it was considered not good enough to be kept for a long period of time because the contents would spoil soon.

Cucumbers were raised for canning in a variety of ways. If we picked a crop of miniature cucumbers early, we made gherkin pickles. Larger cucumbers were made up to be sweet and sour, bread and butter, or dill pickles. The canning of tomatoes was the most work, as they needed to be not only picked but prepared in different ways. Some would be put up as tomato sauce, others as whole tomatoes and some as juice. Each method meant a lot of work. Those same large canning pots, lots of glass jars with lids and rubber seals were needed. The tomatoes were prepared and cooked. The jars were always washed and then boiled with the lids and seals in another pot. The jars were left to cool. Then the process was to fill the jars, put the seals and caps on while warm and leave them to cool and seal.

SCHOOL TIME

"School days, school days
Dear Old Golden Rule days
Reading and 'riting and 'rithmetic
Taught to the tune of the hick'ry stick
You were my queen in calico
I was your bashful, barefoot beau
And you wrote on my slate, "I Love You So
When we were a couple o'kids"

The summers were all too short. Suddenly it was time to go back to school. My grade school was located near McHenry's downtown. Looking back, it was a typical, brick, two story, square building that sat on a hill overlooking downtown.

Along one side of the playground was a creek that was off limits to students. Our playground was blacktop and covered a large area on one side and the back of the building. No fences surrounded the school or the playground. Some grass was across the front on either side of the front entry. The front of the building faced a side street.

The playground had certain areas designated and marked out for hopscotch. I played with friends and it was a good way to test our balance and dexterity to be able to hop on one foot or two. The idea was to get to the other end without touching any of the marked off lines or falling completely outside the borders. If either occurred, we would have to start over.

The girls usually jumped rope and the boys played kick ball or just ran around chasing each other playing tag.

An area was set aside for playground equipment, which consisted of monkey bars, parallel bars and a balance bar set down low to the ground. That bar was wide enough to walk on by putting one foot in front of the other or stepping sideways down the entire length. It wasn't even as wide as our shoes so it became a challenge.

CLASSROOM

Recess and lunch time weren't very long but it gave all of us time to run off some of the stored-up energy after sitting in the classroom.

The classrooms were very typical of the type of school of that era. Blackboards were on three sides of the room and a long bulletin board was on the fourth side. The teacher's desk always sat up front so he or she could watch over every move we made. Around the top of those different boards was a border of the letters of the alphabet all in upper case and lower case print. Because of the postwar construction of school buildings, our school was typical. It was all wood framed with wood used extensively inside. The walls in the hallways and rooms were made and covered with wood.

MR. MIKE, OUR SCHOOL BUS DRIVER

Mr. Mike drove the school bus for years in our area. He knew each and every one of us by name as he lived only a block from my house. There were perhaps eight of us who waited at the side of the street with no shelter from the elements. I'm sure he was always on time for the pickup as he seemed that type of a person. There were never any loud noises coming from us as he always kept us under control with his mild manner. At Christmastime he always had a small present for each and every one of us.

My first day of school was a trip on the school bus with Mr. Mike. My mom was at the bus stop but didn't go to school with me. I was going to be a big boy in front of my playmates. Oh, how I had mixed emotions at the time! I wanted to go to school but at the same time I wanted to stay home. I was all dressed in my new school clothes and shoes. At that time we never had backpacks. My carrying device was a paper bag. My mom and dad had purchased all the required school supplies, so I was all set complete with a bag lunch. I got on the bus, gave a wave to mom and then realized big boys don't cry so I tried to hold back any tears that might form. My teacher was waiting outside the school for each bus to arrive. That first day went well and from that point on school was not so bad after all. After school it was back on the bus and home to lots of hugs and kisses from my mom.

GRADE SCHOOL TEACHERS

All of my teachers were good and at the same time kept anyone who misbehaved in line. The well-known threat was knowing you could be sent to the principal's office. None of us wanted that to happen!

SCHOOL PICNICS

Every grade had a school picnic each year. It was a fun time to take a full size bus and go to one of the city parks located in our town. There were all sorts of games to play. The playgrounds were different than what we had at school. When it was time for lunch, we had brought a brown paper-bag lunch from home. More games were played after lunch and then back to school to be dismissed.

SICKNESS

As a child I rarely got sick and if I did, it was probably a cold. Mom treated a cold by sending me to bed for complete bed rest. If I had a high fever, a cold compress was laid on my head. We all used handkerchiefs so having a cold meant more laundry and ironing for mom. Medicine consisted of an aspirin and lots of orange juice or whole oranges peeled by mom. Hot chicken soup or tomato soup was common practice. Soup didn't fill up my stomach but I survived. There was no running to the doctor or the need for him to make a house call. Mom always treated the cold or fever on the home front. I did catch the measles one year and the chicken pox the next year. Both came in the spring right in time for me to miss the annual school picnic two years in a row. Thank heavens I never had any broken bones.

THE "WEEKLY READER"

When I was in grade school we were given the opportunity to subscribe to a newspaper called the "Weekly Reader" that came out weekly. It was just six pages long on regular paper. It had a wealth of stories, poems, songs and puzzles. I don't recall the cost but my mom made sure I got one each week until I outgrew it in my later school years. I was always excited to get my copy because I enjoyed reading and the little "Weekly Reader" helped open up the world to me.

CLASSROOM SEATING AT SCHOOL

One thing I dreaded at the beginning of each school year was the seating arrangement set down by the teachers. I always knew before I even came into the room to find a seat that even if I sat down either in the middle or the back, I would be called up to the front to sit at the very first desk. Because my last name started with an A the teacher seated us in alphabetical order that very first day. In that way he or she got to know our names and faces. There were times when I would be asked a question first.

I would sweat at those times because I either didn't know the answer or fumbled to think of the answer. Many times I wished my name started with a W or better yet a Z.

BEING LEFT-HANDED IN A RIGHT-HANDED WORLD

When I was learning how to write, my natural way was to hold the pencil in my left hand. That was considered a no no in the school world with not only one but two of my teachers. I never wrote anything with my hand over the top of the letters so I didn't see any need to pick up a pencil and use my right hand. Being left-handed was normal and comfortable for me. I can remember both of these teachers trying from time to time to get me to switch to my right hand for writing but to no avail. I still am left-handed and do very well in right-handed situations or using a right-handed tool. My dad would say my being left-handed came in handy when there were projects that only I could do for the work needed.

BAD WEATHER AND MISSING THE SCHOOL BUS

In those years I must have had a rain coat as I can't imagine that my mother would let me stand in the rain without one. There were never any parents who drove their children in cars to the bus stop because it was just one block from our house. We had to wait in all types of weather and probably looked like drowned ducks in bad weather with our heads bent low. I do remember my mom trying to make me wear a pot cover from the kitchen as a rain hat. NO way would I put that thing on my head! I would never have heard the end of it from the rest of the neighborhood kids. So off we all went to get drenched.

One time for some odd reason we all missed the pickup time or the bus was late. Either way it was decided that we had to walk to school. At that time there were several boys who could be bullies when they wanted to be. Well, that morning they were just that. It was decided that since it was the dead of winter, the shortest way to school was to cross over the river on the ice. The ice was frozen, so off we went, staying well clear of the so-called slushy areas that showed water on the ice and a different color than normal, frozen ice. I didn't know that even if the top was frozen, the water was constantly moving downstream directly under the ice. Well, let me tell you we all got in trouble that day when it was discovered what we had done to get to school. Never again did any of us kids take that short cut to school. The long way was just fine. It was a hike walking the long way but much safer for us.

"School's out, school's out
Teacher let the monkeys out...
No more pencils, no more books
No more teacher's dirty looks..."

SUNDAY SCHOOL

Sunday school was above and beyond regular school. At our church it was held on Sunday morning while the adults were attending the regular church service. The teacher read Bible stories and we had small projects to do to help us learn our Bible lessons each week. I recall looking at the bulletin board in the room to see how many small stars had been posted beside my name. Roll call was taken each week and that was one way to gain another star. There were stars in various colors for perhaps completing a project or memorizing a Bible verse. When it got close to Christmas, we all were given a verse to memorize or perhaps a song to learn for the children's Christmas program.

FALL

LEAVES IN THE FALL

There was a row of trees across the front of our property and at various locations spotted around the entire yard. They were beautiful to see and great for much needed shade during the hot summer. When the leaves came floating down, it was not much fun. Piles and piles of leaves were all hand raked. My dad would let us kids rake them up so we could make pretend houses. All we had to do was rake them and make rows of leaves that became rooms. An entire house could be mapped out with just small piles of leaves in a straight line complete with doorways and windows. We would proceed to play in that house for a while.

Then it was deemed necessary to rake them over to the burning pile. Yes, in those days everyone could burn their leaves. There would be this gray cloud of smoke hanging over everyone's house and perhaps covering the entire town. The wonderful smell of burning leaves was a special memory. One of the most important things to do when we were near a pile of leaves was to jump into them or to walk through them by kicking and shuffling our feet. Lying down in the middle of that pile was also fun to do. The idea was to be covered with the leaves like a blanket.

APPLES

Another important fruit to have on hand in the fall was apples. We didn't have any apple trees that I can remember. I'm sure that my folks got several bushels from friends, my dad's coworkers or from people at church. Certain apples made great applesauce while others were great for just eating. Applesauce was necessary to make and store. There again my mom would wash and prep the apples. It takes quite awhile to peel each apple and cut each one into quarters for cooking. After cooking the apples, they were placed into the jars, sealed and left to cool on the counter. There again we all were delegated the task of listening and counting throughout the evening for each lid to pop. What a good, tasty treat that would be all winter to have a serving of homemade applesauce. This was all thanks to my mom's hard and never ending work.

The canning and preserving of all the garden's bounty was a big job but that canning would help to feed us in the coming winter months and be a welcomed sight on our plates in the dead of winter. The taste was always like none other. FRESH is the magic word!

FARM VISIT - MILKING

One time my parents made arrangements for me to stay overnight with a couple from our church at their small farm. The excitement of that experience was enough for me. It was a working dairy farm that was just on the edge of town. I was excited to go as it meant tagging along with Mr. Higgins as he did his daily chores. I rode with him on the tractor, climbed in and cleaned his huge barn, and helped clean up after the cows. After that day of assorted chores it was late afternoon and time for milking. The milking was done by hand into a bucket.

Before the actual milking, Mr. Higgins had to get the cows into the barn, into their own stanchions and washed up. The cows were in the barnyard already as they had followed the lead cow into that area. The lead cow always came in first with the others following. If you didn't see the lead cow, you could hear the quiet ringing of the bell that hung around its neck. That was the clue that all the herd was slowly coming into the barnyard. Mr. Higgins didn't have automated milking machines as they were too costly for a small farm.

Once the cows were ready to milk, he milked them one by one sitting on a small stool and filling buckets with milk. The milk was then poured into large milk cans and kept overnight in the cool milk house. The next morning that milk was transported by truck to the local dairy.

When the work day was finally over, we had supper, washed up and went to bed. Morning came around real early when I was awakened and had to dress for breakfast. I sat down to a rather ordinary breakfast. The one lasting thought I still have is that the milk I was given to drink came straight from the cows. How I ever got that milk down is beyond me. I never have had that kind of milk since.

FARM VISIT – HAYING TIME

Another time some years later I helped out at haying time. There again I was very excited be a part of that operation on a farm in Wisconsin. I rode on the hay wagon but couldn't lift the heavy bales because of my small size so I was asked to drive the tractor. I did just that after a short lesson in how to drive the tractor. It felt rather strange to drive at slow speed across a field. Every time the baler released another bale, the whole tractor and wagon would jerk. On the wagon the men would have to stand with their legs spread so as not to fall off. It was hot at that time of the year and very dusty. I was relieved when it was lunchtime and we could quit for awhile. I had all these visions in my mind of what was called a hay baler lunch with lots of food, big portions and that would be shared with everyone. Well, lunch consisted of homemade bread, cheese, pickles and milk. That was it! I hope that I didn't show my disappointment to the others.

HALLOWEEN

Halloween always holds a special spot in a child's heart. Mine wasn't any different in that respect. It was almost like Christmas but yet in a different, fun way. Just the thought of dressing up in a costume was enough excitement for any child. In those days all the costumes were put together from discarded items found around the house like an old hat or shirt. Dressing up like an old man with a cane was always a good, traditional kind of outfit. Or I could dress up wearing one of my mom's old dresses, jewelry and an old purse. The costume didn't need to be fancy, just fun enough to try to fool the neighbors. The idea was to not be recognized by anyone.

The treats that were common at Halloween were usually homemade popcorn balls or cookies. The treats were never store bought. Because our neighborhood in McHenry was small, there were not many homes to go to for trick-or-treating. Our treat gathering time was probably less than an hour.

Now if "trick" was the thought at the moment, the tradition was to carry a bar of soap just in case a homeowner didn't give out a treat. Actually, I don't think I ever soaped a window but I still had the bragging rights for just bringing along the soap.

At school the teachers would do something special with a little party and treats like cupcakes, cookies and drinks brought in by a room mother. All in all, a good time was had by all at that time of year.

WILD FOWL IN THE SWAMP

Because of my love and appreciation of nature and the outdoors, from time to time in the fall I would go to the swamp to watch the ducks and geese. They would land there to rest before continuing their flight south to spend the winter. While they were resting, it was a perfect time for me to sit on the shore, watch and observe the various types, shapes and colors of the birds. Their migration always took place each year as the weather was too cold and the winter was too long. Besides, the water would freeze over even on the river. There was too much snow cover for them to find food.

The flight of geese in the sky above could be heard for miles before finally the flock appeared. My mind was mystified by the simple fact that geese always flew in a V-shaped pattern with one goose leading the entire flock. Those sights and sounds fascinated me and I was in awe watching them fly overhead.

Nowadays the weather has changed so dramatically that most of the rivers remain open so that migration has not only changed but has almost ended.

BARBERSHOP

There were several barber shops in town but my dad always used the same one. It was another of the local meeting places for men just to stop in to chat or to get a haircut or a shave. The barber knew people by their first names. I would be waiting my turn and at the same time listening to their conversations. There was a table filled with magazines and newspapers. My dad knew a lot of people so the talk was always lively. I was in awe when the barber would shave one of the men. I would watch him sharpen the straight razor on a strap that hung off the side of the chair. Then he removed the hot towels from the man's face and applied the lather. Shaving cream was not in aerosol cans but soap in a small mug with a brush. If one of the regulars got a shave all the time, a mug was set aside just for him. Then the barber carefully moved the very sharp razor back and forth to remove the whiskers.

UNCLE WALTER AT FAMILY THANKSGIVING DINNER

After a huge Thanksgiving dinner at my Aunt Pearl and Uncle Walter's house in the city, it was time to clear the table and wash the many dishes. The women were obviously all busy trying to clear the table when my Uncle Walter announced from the living room, "Why don't you put all the dishes in the bathtub and wash them in there?" The bathroom was on the way to the kitchen so it just seemed the thing to do, according to him. After the laughter quieted down, the women went back to carrying the dishes beyond the bathroom to the kitchen. All dishwashing was done by hand and dried individually with dish towels.

WINTER

SNOWFLAKES

My dad somehow got our big yard ready for snow and the shovels ready for snow shoveling. When the first snow fell, I would go outside and try to catch the snowflakes in my open, upturned hand. I tried to see the flakes and study each one before it melted. Did you know that the claim is that no two snowflakes are the same? I could stick my tongue out and hope a snowflake would fall on my tongue to instantly melt there. I probably looked rather funny standing with my head pointed up and my mouth open. Who cares, right? Only a child can do that type of thing and not be laughed at by others.

DRESSING TO GO OUTDOORS TO PLAY IN THE SNOW

As the snow piled up, it was time to put on my boots, heavy coat, scarf and hat to go outside and romp in the falling snow. All those items were watched over by mom and had to be put on before I could go outside. Sometimes I had so many clothes on I couldn't move very freely but I went outside anyway. In my mind I needed to hurry so that I could get outside right away. When I was small, my mom always tied a scarf across my mouth so I didn't breathe in cold air. How could I go out and play when I felt that I could hardly breathe? Somehow and sometime later the scarf always came off when mom was not looking and it was discarded. However, I realized that when I came back in mom would say the magical words, "Where's your scarf and why don't you have it on?"

Then I was finally ready to fling open the door. At that point I was so excited I didn't know what to do first. Should I run, jump, fall down and roll, make snowballs or join in snowball throwing contests with the other kids? After the newness started to wear off, I could pick and choose how to play in the snow.

SNOW ANGELS AND FROST ON THE WINDOWS

One thing I really enjoyed was to lie down in the fresh snow and make snow angels. They were easy. All I had to do was lie flat on my back in the fresh snow and move my arms and legs in full arcs up and down and sideways, thus creating what looked like an angel with spread wings. The trick was to carefully get up slowly and not to disturb the pattern I had just formed.

If I happened to be inside, I could always go to a window and see how the frost had created the most beautiful patterns on the glass. The frost patterns took on all kinds of shapes and the patterns were never the same again. Frost on a window and snowflakes are some of the remarkable creations of nature.

SLEDDING

Two doors from my house lived the Johnson family. I have previously written that the father had brought home the first TV in the neighborhood. They also had a piece of property alongside their house with ground that sloped at just the right angle to make a perfect sledding hill. It was not too long and not too steep. Just right! We would spend hours out on that hill. We would walk up and sled down over and over. We always had to be careful not to walk on the actual run area as it would beat down and disturb the snow. One big thing was that we would race against each other. The idea was to be at the top, someone would yell "go" and then we would run and flop onto our sled while at a full run. We all enjoyed that so much that after an afternoon we would go home to warm up.

I always dried off the sled's runners to make sure they didn't rust. It was a little trick given to me by my dad. Then a little of dad's machine oil was spread over the runners and I was good to go the next day. The whole idea was to be the best and have the fastest sled. The name brand of my sled was the "American Flyer." The sled was about four feet long with two runners and handles on the front by which to steer with either your feet if sitting or by your arms if lying down. Either way worked just fine!

Author With His Sled

SNOW FORTS

Snow forts were always being built around our neighborhood. We needed the protection of that wall if there was a snowball fight starting or going on. It was just snow blocks or rather large snowballs rolled and placed together. Nothing fancy but just plain protection so that we had a place to duck behind to get away from the snowballs coming our way.

96

IGLOO

I remember once being part of the building team to create an igloo. As kids we felt we had graduated to building one as we always built snow forts for snowball fights so this igloo was going to be a work of art. The snow in the yard was just right and had frozen over on the top so all we had to do was to cut the snow into blocks. Then we brought the blocks over to the construction area and stacked one on top of the other. As in bricklaying they were placed just right and our igloo took shape. The idea was to stack each row a little more towards the center so the igloo would have a tapered roof with just a hole at the top. After a lot of snow blocks and hard work we achieved our mission. A small entryway was created for the doorway. After it was completed, there wasn't anything to do but to crawl in and sit in the middle of the room. I'm sure the igloo lasted for some days as our winters then were very cold. Our igloo was a monument to all of us at the time.

SNOWBALL INCIDENT AT CHURCH

One time I was at our church on a Saturday for some kid's activity and we were given a recess. It was winter and there was a lot of good packing snow on the ground. The group decided to toss snowballs around, which became a snowball fight. I got involved and soon was an active thrower of snowballs. I had just made a perfect ball and had another kid in my sight as the target. That kid was on the front steps leading into the church. Well, he moved aside just as I let my snowball fly. That ball not only was on a direct path to the front doors but went through them when someone opened the door at the same time. That snowball rolled right down the center isle and ended up near the front of the church's altar. Boy, was I in trouble then! All I could say was that I was sorry and would clean up the now melting snowball. My lesson for the day: Accidents will happen but they should not happen in the church.

INSIDE ACTIVITIES

After being outside for quite some time, I had to come in to get dry and warm. A change of clothes was the first item of business. If I didn't do it for myself right away, my mom made sure that I changed out of my cold, wet clothes. Then perhaps a cup of hot chocolate was in order. LISTENING TO THE RADIO

One of the things that I reflect on was going upstairs to my big bedroom and turning on the radio. It was a large unit with its own cabinet for not only the radio but also a record player. I was fascinated by the tuning bar that showed different settings. It had not only regular channels but also broadband. I think it was connected to an antenna and I could actually have heard from other parts of the world. All

I could do was listen and be excited about what that radio could receive.

At that time all I wanted to do was hear my favorite programs like the "The Lone Ranger" and his sidekick Tonto, "Gene Autry," "Hopalong Cassidy" and "Call of the Wild." At Christmastime there was a program called "The Cinnamon Bear." "The program is meant to be heard once per day between November 29 and Christmas Eve."

"The Cinnamon Bear, episode #1: 'Paddy O'Cinnamon"

**"Judy and Jimmy write letters to Santa.
The Silver Star Christmas ornament is missing
And the kids go up to the attic to find it.
They meet Paddy O'Cinnamon (The Cinnamon Bear)
Who tells them the Silver Star was taken to
Maybeland by the Crazy Quilt Dragon."**

Late in the afternoon around 5:00 I would lie down in front of the set and listen to the stories unfold. Each day a new story was told complete with sound effects. What a great lead up to Christmas!

CHRISTMAS TIME

As seen through the eyes of any child, Christmas was just plain fascinating in so many ways. Our house was all decorated with a freshly cut tree with all of the ornaments, lights and tinsel. Tinsel was rather long, thin strands of silver, ribbon type material laid over the ends of each branch. It gave the visual effect of snow on the tree and would sparkle when the lights were turned on. When the tree was taken down after Christmas, that tinsel was saved and put back on a cardboard holder for next year. In those years nothing went to waste nor was thrown away. Everything was saved and packed away in storage to be used again and again.

Under that same tree presents would start to show up but they were only the ones not from Santa. Santa's packages, all neatly wrapped and sorted, magically appeared on Christmas Eve while we were at church. I never did figure out for some years how Santa could get into our locked house. My mom might have had something to do with that as she was always the last one to come out and get into the car.

GOING TO CHURCH ON CHRISTMAS EVE

Our family's tradition was going to church on Christmas Eve. I was part of the Sunday school program and the children's portion of the service was to tell the Christmas story out loud up in front of the congregation. We all sat on small chairs and faced the congregation and then stood up when it was our turn to say our part of the story. Perhaps that was the origin of the phrase "saying your piece." I was probably a nervous wreck as were many others. Somehow we all got through our piece and then there were songs to be sung, prayers and a short message from the minister. When we were dismissed, we marched out of the church and each one of us received a paper bag filled with an apple, an orange and some hard candy. When we arrived home, I would charge into the living room to see if Santa

Claus had come. Oh, yes, he never forgot our house with help from my mom and dad, I'm sure.

One thing that remains in my memory is what I saw on the roof one year. In those years there was always snow at Christmas. I looked up and saw what seemed to be the markings of a sleigh runner on the back side of the roof peak. It was dark but I could just barely make out one mark. It was about six feet long but I was sure it was from Santa's sleigh. There again I never figured out how that single mark got there and my dad, with a big smile on his face, didn't know either.

CHRISTMAS PRESENTS

Our Christmas presents to each other were given with love and were simple, needed items. My mom and dad gave each other a pair of pajamas and a pair of slippers. My mom would also get a box of "Fannie Mae" candy. Dad would buy a card and give it to mom. My dad received a book, which was always signed on the front cover by my mom. Dad also received a box of handkerchiefs because he carried one each and every day.

I would make something at school or in the workshop at home for each of my parents. Those were the gifts that they cherished the most. I would be given pajamas, slippers and a toy, a special game or a book. Sometimes another piece of clothing was needed. Mrs. Santa Claus always made sure we each received a plate of goodies, fruits and nuts.

One of my favorite Christmas gifts was a Lionel train set. It was a set consisting of a locomotive, a coal car and three or four passenger cars. They were made of metal and were very detailed in not only the painting but the fact that the doors on the cars actually opened. The set was wired internally so when the train was running the cars would all light up. There also were small capsules that were placed in the smokestack of the locomotive. When the engine got hot enough, the capsules would melt and fire off the effect of smoke. The set had all the other necessary components like the tracks, switches and a transformer. Because it was a Christmas present, I found it still in the box all wrapped up with a big bow. I was thrilled beyond words so my dad and I set it up in my upstairs bedroom. From then on that winter I played with it over and over. The track later was mounted on a sheet of plywood and stayed on my bedroom floor so the track would remain stationary. I used and played with that train set for many years to come.

CAR RIDES AND TRIPS

SUNDAY DRIVE

Sunday was a day of rest. We went to church in the morning, then usually home. My mom prepared a noon meal and if we had no company coming over, we would go for a ride. My mom never learned how to drive, so getting out like that was a treat for her. It was never a long drive and my dad's goal always was to seek out an ice cream soda. In his mind it had to be a soda and nothing else. We would all order the same thing. Over the years it became harder and harder to find the shop or soda fountain that still made sodas. When we couldn't find one, our order would be double dipped ice cream in a sugar cone. In those days the dips were generous in size so on a hot day it became a challenge to eat it before it melted and was running down our arms. My dad had a difficult time accepting the fact that sodas weren't made anymore. Lots of soda fountains discontinued using pressurized seltzer water, which was the one and only ingredient besides the ice cream. As I got bigger, I wanted a milk shake instead of a cone. My dad eventually went along with my choice.

LONG RIDES

As any parent can remember, when going on a trip, the child or children would always say those magical words, "Are we there yet?" or "Can we eat now?" I wasn't any different. My mom always packed sandwiches and fruit in a metal picnic basket for lunch time. We did not stop at restaurants to eat a meal. When I was bored with the driving, I would ask the question, "Are we close to town?" At that moment my dad would tell me to look for a roadside rest area as the next town was close after that roadside rest area. Nine chances out of ten we didn't stop at that roadside. If I did see one, dad just kept driving. The next town was not close by any means. It took me several years to realize I was being tricked by the simple fact that roadsides are put out in the middle of nowhere and not near a town. That's why they are called rest areas.

AMPHITHEATER

My folks took me into Chicago to the Amphitheater next to the stock yards on the near South Side of Chicago to see several of my heroes in person. That very large building in a major city over a year's time had a vast variety of shows. Going to such a place and seeing my favorite heroes was a treat beyond my wildest boyhood dreams. To see a TV personality even from a distance was awesome to say the least. Our seats were usually high up in the balconies but I didn't care. After a show in the main arena these same heroes of mine would ride around the outer edge so we could see them up close.

I can still remember the numerous small booths in the corridors and even sellers carrying a large bunch of pennants and hand held souvenirs. On their heads they would have a whole stack of cowboy hats. Yes, a whole stack so you could pick out whichever one you wanted right on the spot. They were called hawkers because they would call out their products in a very high, loud voice to get your attention so that you would buy from them and not from someone else.

GOING TO THE ZOO

Going to Brookfield Zoo was a special trip. We had lots of walking and lots of sights to see with all the animals, birds and reptiles all in their natural environment and surroundings. It was a great experience for my mom, dad and me to share.

WYOMING TRIP

Author Standing Next To "Entering Wyoming" Sign

After the Second World War, when gas was readily available once again, my parents decided to take a trip west to Yellowstone National Park in Wyoming. We packed, loaded the trunk and the three of us took off in our car. Vacations were always the driving type and our car was in good shape to make the long trip. I was excited to go on this trip as I had visions of seeing cowboys and the western plains. Driving through Iowa was boring with countless miles of nothing but field after field of corn and soybeans. When we got to Nebraska, there were more innumerable miles of flat fields and nothing to see. Then into Wyoming and we finally saw the hills and mountains. The scenery had changed so now I was intent on seeing cowboys on horses.

The places we stayed at night were always small individual cabins set in a grouping. At that time you could pick out a motel with multiple rooms under one roof but my dad preferred a cabin. The cabins were small in size and only had room for two beds, a table and several chairs. The bathrooms were also small. Several outdoor chairs sat near the front door. All the cabins we stayed at were nothing fancy but they were clean. Most had a courtyard that you drove on to get to your cabin. Usually a grassy area in that courtyard had more chairs and tables for relaxing.

**Author And
Mom In Front
Of Cabin**

There also was no breakfast, lunch or dinner available on site. We had to go elsewhere to eat. It usually was not too far since we were always on a major highway. I remember at one of the cabins where we stayed someone had ponies that could be ridden right there. It was such a thrill because I had never ridden a pony or horse before. I still have a picture of me sitting on that pony with the biggest smile you can imagine. I was all decked out in my cowboy hat, boots and holster with my gun. Boy, did I feel grown up at that moment!

I can recall my dad driving through open country and suddenly coming upon a large group of locusts that were crossing the road. My dad stopped for a moment and decided to drive right over those bugs. There was no way to drive around them so he just drove over them. There were so many that they became a plague to the farmers as locusts would eat anything in their path.

We arrived at Cody, Wyoming, which was called the gateway to Yellowstone Park. There again we stayed in a cabin. Due to the altitude it was cold late in the afternoon and it got even colder during the night. One item on our agenda while we were in town was to go to a real rodeo. We put on every bit of clothing we had brought on the trip just to stay warm. The thrill of seeing that rodeo is a memory beyond words.

During the day we did some window shopping. The next day we were driving on to Yellowstone. It was fantastic and almost magical. Buffaloes were standing in the middle of the road without a care in the world. I had never seen such enormous, strange looking animals roaming the roads. The more we drove, the more signs we saw stating, "Don't feed the bears." Lo and behold, we came upon some bears actually stopping traffic to beg for food. Some people would actually get out of their cars to feed them. However, they soon realized they better not do that and retreated back to their cars. The cuteness of the situation changed quickly.

After driving for some time, we finally came upon the main lodge. It was a beautiful, log building. I heard someone say they were wondering about what appeared to be a scuttle hole in the roof, which was over the second floor balcony. The response from a forest ranger was it would be the only way to get in or out of the building during the winter. The snow could be so deep that it blocked the doors on ground level. I guess that no one lived there but they did need a way to check on the building. Can you imagine so much snow that you couldn't shovel your way to the door? That got my attention even as a young boy.

After touring the lodge, my dad checked us in and we proceeded on to our cabin. I can still remember that the inside was very plain. The cabin was of log construction and had a log fireplace. The part that surprised me the most was that the beds were unusually high off the floor. We actually had to use stools to get up and into bed. We hoped we wouldn't fall out during the night and break or bruise something. The reason the beds were so high was because it was warmer closer to the ceiling since heat rises. We couldn't cook in the cabin so we had to get freshened up and go to the main lodge for breakfast.

Breakfast ended up being a real treat for all of us and all of the other customers. It seems that a young deer would make its rounds to all the windows that faced the woods. The deer was given the name "Minnie the Mooch." That deer came up to every window begging for food by just staring at everyone. "Minnie" would get something to eat and then move on to the next window to repeat the process again and again.

The next day we went out to where the geyser "Old Faithful" was located. The history about that geyser was that it spouted out a very high cloud of steam from far below the surface. The ironic part was I stayed on a bench located near the geyser hole but my dad wanted to get closer. He set down his "Brownie" snapshot camera next to me before leaving the bench. When the geyser started to erupt, I got excited and must have touched the trigger on the camera. I proceeded, by accident, to get a picture of the eruption at half its full height. The best part of it was I didn't know I had taken it until sometime later when the film was developed. It turned out to be a great picture!

Another thing that comes to mind is that a lot of the people who took a driving vacation had to show off where they had visited. That information was in the form of a sticker you bought and put in a window of your car. It would be nothing to see cars with multiple stickers from all over the United States.

PENNANTS

Felt pennants that I could hang on my bedroom wall were also popular. They were printed and detailed with a favorite personality or there were pennants from every state that could be purchased. The state pennants usually were bought on a trip rather then found in the local dime store. They were souvenirs to be brought home from a trip.

MISCELLANEOUS RECOLLECTIONS

CEREAL BOX WITH PRIZES, GAMES

Breakfast food advertising by major companies was big and still is to this day. I wasn't any different in the fact that when I sat down at the table, I would reach out for my favorite cereal box and while eating I would try to read the back of the box. On that box was a vast amount of not only games I could play but also quizzes, puzzles and items that I could purchase. All I needed to do was save a specified amount of box tops and perhaps some coins or currency. I sent my box tops and coins so I could have a special ring that was offered. That ring when it arrived in the mailbox would fit my finger and stick up above it by perhaps a half an inch. Due to the size it then could be unfolded and it had all kinds of things inside like an ink pen, a magnifying glass or a secret compartment for storage. The ring wasn't that all fired big but as a boy I thought I had something to wear that was extra special!

Some of the radio and TV stars that I watched or listened to offered prizes that I could send away for. One was a special drink cup with the star's name plastered all over it alongside the name of the product that you would be drinking at the same time. One brand was "Ovaltine." That was a premixed, chocolate powder that was added to milk and then heated. A picture of the main character was on the outside of the cup. The idea behind the promotional cup was we could buy that product over and over.

There also were cereal bowls set up in the same way. A great promotional tool for the product manufacturer was to keep their name in print in front of you, especially for children. Then I wanted to eat my cereal in the special bowl. I can attest that I had, thanks to my mom's help, a certain number of those little treasures throughout my childhood.

DAIRIES

There was a local dairy in town that processed all of the area's milk. I grew up in an age when the local dairy handled all the milk and milk by-products for McHenry. A family could buy milk at a grocery store, at the dairy or have home delivery. After the war, home delivery was becoming increasingly popular with families. All of the milk came only in glass bottles. They were of assorted sizes depending on which product it was and the bottles were sealed with little paper caps.

I'm reminded of the fact that seeing the actual bottle sitting on the table for a meal meant it was my chore to keep the empty bottles in one spot at the back door so they could be returned. The bottles were then returned to the dairy or to the store and the bottles were washed by the dairy to be used again and again.

BASEBALL CARDS

Baseball cards have been around since before my childhood but I was made aware of them when the neighborhood kids showed them to me. I was told that I could buy them at the small neighborhood store or at the dime store in town. I proceeded to check them out and bought a few for myself and perhaps to trade. I never really followed baseball that much at the time so I didn't know who the well-known players were. I collected them just to be part of the group.

COMIC BOOKS

As a boy I had the opportunity to purchase and read comic books. They were readily available in many of the local stores. Many of the characters that I knew and loved on radio and TV were now in comic books. The books were ten cents each. I would purchase one, bring it home and proceed to look at it countless times. My stack of books grew so I always had something to read.

Now those same comic books are collector's items and worth a fair amount of money if they are in mint condition. Would we ever have thought that comic books would be worth so much money in later years?

A FLUTE MADE FOR ME

One time my folks were invited to go to the home of one of my dad's coworker's. Their place was east of town and they lived next to a small lake. Frank, my dad and I took a walk after supper and we ended up next to some tall cane stalks. Frank took out his knife and cut off a portion of one of the hollow canes. He then cut holes at various locations along one side and thus created an instant flute. He gave it to me right then and I was thrilled. He also showed me at the same time how to make another flute with the outer shell sliding like a trombone. I kept those flutes for some years to come. A simple musical instrument made from a length of cane growing along the water's edge!

DAD AND UNCLE BEN WITH CONTINUING CONVERSATIONS ABOUT THE BEST CAR TO OWN

I came across a picture of my dad standing next to Uncle Ben and that photo brought back a memory. When my dad and Uncle Ben were together to talk, the

**Dad on the left
and Uncle Ben**

conversation eventually turned to cars. For years my dad always drove GM products. Most of them were Pontiacs. My uncle on the other hand always drove Chryslers. If Uncle Walter was also present, we all would hear his praises for the Studebaker. My dad and Uncle Ben constantly had this conversation. They would go back and forth trying to convince each other to switch brands. It was a standoff each time as neither one would admit the other might be right and have the best car.

That conversation continued for many years. As a boy I would honor my dad and uncle by listening but after awhile I realized it would just be a draw again. The ironic thing was that my dad's last car was a Chrysler. It took years but Uncle Ben finally won. Dad loved his Chrysler.

BIRTHDAYS

Birthdays were always special and my mom would make a special dinner for each of us on our birthdays. We did not go to restaurants to pay for a meal. All our parties were at home and consisted of dinner, a cake with candles glowing, singing the 'Happy Birthday' song and a few presents. There again it was simple but always done and shared with love for that person on their special day.

THE IMPORTANCE OF SAVING

Looking back to my childhood days, I am reminded of what both my parents instilled in me over and over. It was the importance of saving my money. Yes, I have previously mentioned the quarter my grandmother gave me and how it would buy an ice cream cone. As a young boy I did like everyone else and spent it almost right away. Then my parents showed me how to save that first quarter from grandmother and add it to the next quarter that she would give me. Now my savings totaled fifty cents. My folks told me how important it was to not spend money on something that would be gone in minutes. They set up a savings fund for me at home. Every once in awhile they would give me a portion of my savings to spend but the balance was saved. Dad told me that Ben Franklin said, "A penny saved is a penny earned." Another of Dad's sayings was, "A dollar feels real good staying right here in my pocket" and "if you can't afford to pay for something that is not within your budget, then you don't need it."

CLINTON, WISCONSIN

We moved to Clinton, Wisconsin to fulfill my dad's dream of owning his own print shop. Little did I know then that my parent's savings plan would allow them to do this. My mom and dad bought and operated their own newspaper. It was a very small business and served only the surrounding farm area. The advertisements in the paper paid the bills and dad depended on the success of the paper for our livelihood.

He went out to sell the current week's ads and gather up next week's ads, and came back to the shop to set them all up for print. A major job! He operated the printing press, which was not automatic. Each sheet was hand fed into the press. Nothing really happened in that small community, so the news was only a small portion of the paper. My dad even printed all of the minutes from the local meetings. It was of some use to the readers but as my dad would say, time and time again, "It doesn't put bread and butter on the table." There wasn't any money to be had from publishing those weekly meeting minutes in the paper but they were important for the readers to be informed. With a limited subscription base, he could count on only a small amount of revenue each week. The only thing my father did not do was work on the Linotype machine. With that machine the operator typed in the news on a keyboard, then the machine turned out actual bars of type that were set into holders that held the individual sheets for the press. He employed a young woman to do that job but she decided from time to time that she wasn't going to come in to work and therefore didn't show up.

Newspapers are run totally on a schedule and each week the schedule remains the same because the print run was always on Thursday. Dad couldn't skip a day due to that rigid schedule. My mom did all the paperwork and accounting, subscriptions, sorting, folding and watching the front desk.

I don't recall how long we lived in Clinton but it couldn't have been too long. Finally, after much worry, pressure and frustration, my dad's longtime dream faded before his eyes. It was just too much for both of them. I still think that if I had been older, perhaps I could have helped and things might have turned out differently but I was just a boy. When thinking back, I realize that the demise of that newspaper took some of the spark out of my dad's completing and fulfilling his dream.

BARRINGTON, ILLINOIS

We moved to Barrington, Illinois because my dad had started a new job with the local newspaper called the "Barrington Press." I'm sure that my dad saw the opportunity to improve his working career. I don't know how he found the time to apply for the job in Barrington but somehow he did it. At the same time he had to sell the business in Clinton and find housing for his family.

OUR HOME IN BARRINGTON

Our home in Barrington was brand new. It was built by a local contractor on the south end of town. The streets at that time were gravel with no curbs, gutters or sidewalks. It was a one story Cape Cod style with a big side yard. The house had two bedrooms, one bath but no central air-conditioning. Our home was one of the first houses in the neighborhood and was surrounded mostly with open fields of grass. The area slowly built up as more and more different styles of homes were added by an assortment of home builders. One unique part of the house was that all the walls were drywall constructed but with two layers of drywall, not one. That was a new concept at that time in home building. Most of the homes were built with plaster prior to that time. The extra layer of drywall would then be equal to the thickness of plaster.

We had an empty field directly across the road which was all tall prairie grass. There were times when I would go across the street and find a spot where the grass was long and thick. I would lie down in that grass and just look up to watch the clouds drift by. It was fun to find a figure or shape in those clouds and just enjoy the clouds moving slowly across the sky. How peaceful that time was for me!

Basically, I just wanted to be outside every chance I got regardless of the time of year. That still holds true for me today. Outdoors there were so many smells, sounds of birds singing and the wind blowing through the trees. In the winter, with snow falling directly down on me, I held out my hand to catch a snowflake.

SOD CUTTING

Our new house didn't have any grass in the yard. It had been prepared somewhat by the builder but it was up to us to put in the grass and do the landscaping. There was a new sidewalk from the gravel street up to the house. My dad decided that he wanted to put sod across the front width of the house. I first had to help my dad finish raking the ground so that it was smooth and ready for the sod. Of course, we couldn't afford to buy sod so I was given a job. I was to take my red "American Flyer" wagon down to the end of the street and dig up the grass sod from a vacant lot. It was wild grass so it wasn't really the quality of grass we wanted but it was free. I would dig it up into squares and bring it to our yard in the wagon. I still have that wagon to-day and it's still in good shape to continue hauling a variety of items. Then the sod was stacked in the yard. I waited for my dad to come home from work so that he and I could lay that sod down. It was constantly watered for days so that the roots would take hold. The rest of the yard was seeded. That same area at the end of the street where I had dug up the sod became a good place to go ice skating in the winter. There was always enough water runoff to collect and then freeze during the winter.

FLOWERS FOR OUR YARD

I had located irises growing in an open field on my way home from school. I told my folks that evening and my dad said, "Take your wagon and dig some up to bring home to transplant for your mom in her large garden." I probably brought home two or three large groupings in my wagon. Then with the help of my dad they were planted and watered. Along with the sod and planting, that's how I learned to work at a young age. I didn't realize at the time but I have worked hard all my life using the simple training I got from dad, which was a big part of my work ethics over the years.

PLANTING BUSHES AND TREES

My dad constantly worked to upgrade the yard. The first year it was to put in trees and bushes at various locations around the yard. Below a shallow layer of black dirt was a layer of clay. That material was almost as hard as rock when I tried to dig a hole for a bush or tree. The digging tools consisted of several shovels, a pick and a pry bar to remove the stones. Each hole took quite some time to prepare and a lot of effort on my part. I still was a young boy but my dad couldn't dig due to his age so I did most of it. Sometimes the clay was so hard I had to let water sit in the hole overnight just to loosen up the soil for the shovel. Somehow we got every flower and bush planted.

My dad decided to build a brick fireplace on a concrete slab. The fireplace was complete with a grill, chimney and wood storage area. I mixed all the mortar and he laid the brick. I mixed all the concrete for the slab foundation by hand in a wheelbarrow. I not only learned concrete work but also bricklaying. We had no outside paid help.

PICKET FENCE

The next project was 200 feet of picket fence to create a fenced yard area. I really don't know how long the actual fence was but I can say there were lots of posts, horizontal rails, posts and pickets. Piles and piles of precut pickets first had to be primed and then assembled. The post holes had to be dug by hand with no power augers available to use in that hard ground. It was a monumental task but there was nothing that my dad and I couldn't do or wouldn't tackle. After the fence had been completed, I was given the task the next summer to apply the finish coat of paint to what we had constructed the previous year. I was told by my dad that I could take all summer to do the painting but he wanted it done by school time. The deal was that I could go swimming or play before or after my work each day. My dad wasn't unreasonable with me but I was creating my own set of work ethics. I still can see that fence in my dreams, painting it almost every day all summer long.

During that same summer, for a rainy day project I was given a full bucket of framing nails that needed to be straightened. My dad had a workshop in the basement and a large vise. My job was to straighten them by means of a hammer for rough and then in the vise for the final bending.

All of the above mentioned jobs were for me to not only help my dad but to teach me good and lasting work habits. I was never in any kind of trouble so it wasn't punishment.

BARRINGTON GRADE SCHOOL

The grade school was located on Hough Street. It was a two story building with a high roof. The exterior was brick with wood framed construction throughout the entire inside. This type of construction was typical of how many schools were built in those years. The stairs were also wood framed and on the second floor there were two metal covered chutes. They were beyond the stairs to provide an escape route for the students. Every so often we would have a fire drill for the entire school. We never knew if there actually was a fire or not because information was not given ahead of time. When we were outside the building, we lined up in rows by class. We didn't have to stand outside too long until everyone and every class was out of the building and the all clear was given. Then we went back inside for the rest of the regular school day. One good thing about having a drill was that some of us enjoyed using the chute. We jumped in feet first and sliding down was a short thrill. After school we would try to climb up the inside of the chute from the bottom.

WALKING TO SCHOOL

I always walked to grade school, which was about six blocks away, in all kinds of weather. My dad was already at work and my mom didn't drive so I had no choice but to walk. While walking to and from school, I enjoyed singing, humming or whistling a song. When I arrived home, my mom would tell me that she could hear me coming by my singing.

SQUIRT GUNS

One time in the spring some of my classmates at school decided we should buy small hand held squirt guns. We all bought them at lunchtime rather than after school. It was fairly easy because the dime store was only a block away. We could easily get there and back during lunch. I have no idea what we were thinking or what would happen when we got back to school and started to go inside. Somehow the word had gotten back to our teacher and to the principal. You can guess who met us at the door. That's right! All of the water pistols were collected and we never saw them again. We got off with a warning. What can I say except, "Boys will be boys."

CONCLUSION

After noting and writing about my childhood, which was fairly typical of that time, I find myself at this point. Even the simple fact that I was raised in a different era doesn't change beliefs and shouldn't change the family unit. It was a much slower and more carefree life then but also much more genuine and wholesome. We lived a simple lifestyle as we believed in the family unit as a whole and in God. We were comfortable, we had food on the table and clothes on our backs, and as my dad would say, "What else does a person need?"

Now we all should be very concerned about where the current generation is going. We have heard about the "me" generation, then it was the "me-me" generation and now it's the "me-me-me" generation. Meaning everyone wants it now and everything needs to be faster and better in their lives. As adults and elders, we find that to be true even while driving with our communication devices of all sorts and in our conversations. Why are we all hurrying? What's at the other end that is so important that it can't wait? Is that call or text message so important that it has to be taken right away? Consequently, you are ignoring the person who is standing right in front of you and talking to you. I have heard other people say that when their family gathers together, someone should collect all the devices and leave them at the back door. I think it's a great idea! Then family and friends could just talk the old-fashioned way. You could see the person's face and be able to read their eyes and expressions.

After the Second World War ended, families were re-united and began to settle down, we found that electronics began to be developed. We were experiencing the birth of the Electronic Age. The computer came into being and that started a revolution of development, first in the business world and then into our personal lives. Now computers run and control a great deal of our everyday lives. Also, when those units go down or crash, become infected with viruses or are hacked, people are just plain lost. Without this one invention people may actually need to carry on a real conversation or use paper and pen. We now can even subscribe to a newspaper on line to catch up on the news. Next we will have a chip put under our skin so we won't even need to carry a unit with us.

Now it's nothing to find small children with a phone, a TV, a computer, an iPod or any number of gaming devices too numerous to mention. Why on earth does a young child of that age need these items? At that age they should be learning how to read, write and develop skills of all sorts. Do most parents properly monitor what their children see and hear? Soon children learn that when they twitch one finger, another screen and item appears to entertain them. They don't need a manual because all they have to do is touch the screen with their finger. Then what? What have they found and how does it help their everyday learning? As one prominent person said, "They are not developing their own personality at all." It's given to them by a machine or a TV set. Have you seen the kids of today doing any of the activities that I did as a child? Making fun for themselves with simple things like a sandbox, a tire swing, leaves piled up, snow angels? I bet not! Young children have a brain like a sponge that can soak up vast amounts of knowledge. The age of reasoning for a child starts about the age of seven so they become open to anything around them from that point on. If it's not monitored, what have parents given that child? A unit that they carry with them all day and consequently not develop their own creativity and interests? How have we as parents taken control of their TV watching?

For a long time, we as the elders have watched the children zone out in front of a TV, and they never hear a thing beyond what is on the screen. It has been used as a babysitter so the parents can move around more freely. I have seen countless children using those units all day long and adults the same way. Are the children learning anything of value? Are they looking up the spelling of a word or checking a math problem? Are they using their own imagination and creativity? I think not! It is just nonsense and drivel. Even adults, you would never have imagined using one, are now on it constantly. For what purpose? That child or adult can't even talk with you at the same time because all of them are so engrossed in that moment. Why do you think that hand held phones should be outlawed from being used while driving a car? Too much distraction! The brain really can't handle two things at the same time with total concentration on the most important issues at hand.

Another thought to ponder: remember what the founders of this country wanted and gave to us, The Declaration of Independence. They kept God in their everyday life and wanted that to be understood by all. "In God We Trust" is on our coins, currency and some public buildings to remind us each and every day.

From the beginning of our country, our soldiers fought to keep us free and countless thousands have died for our flag and our country.

Another major area of vast concern to the older generation is that we have lost or are losing the family unit. "Home is where the heart is." Parents teach us our faith, how to love, how to be humble, how to carry on family traditions and how to be true to ourselves and to others. We don't gather together nearly as much as in years past because everyone is too busy.

I mentioned before about receiving a quarter and what it meant to me and others my age. Well, now, I grant you the monetary value has dropped considerably but it should still be looked upon as something to save. Now the children of today don't want that single quarter unless it's a big bag of quarters. The children want the newest toys or games that cost big money.

The value of our money has dropped. We seem to have no thought or inclination to save it for a rainy day or for future needs. We still have time to slow down our lives and of those around us. We need to teach our children, who are the future of this great country, its true values. Many past generations of everyone's family have sacrificed greatly to teach, to save, to serve and to provide. And let us never forget our parents and grandparents who were part of this country's "Greatest Generation."

Practice what we have been taught and put it to use in our everyday adult lives. Carry on the "faith of our fathers." Honor the flag! Be proud to be an American. Take time to give a smile or a sincere hug, or bend over to hug a child. Remember the saying "in order to get a smile, you need to give one first." Be genuine. Be truthful. Be honest. Be humble. Give. Share. Comfort others. "Pay it again forward." "Your words are windows to your heart." How true and so simple! Try to slow down a bit and try to embrace a more old-fashioned lifestyle. Take time to smell the roses, breathe in that fresh air, watch a bird fly overhead or perhaps gaze at a cloud, rolling gently by overhead. You'll be a better person starting right now if you do. I know you will. Make memories today for yourself and for others but always remember to reminisce and to hold on to the traditions from your past.

Now you have read all of my memories and experiences as a child, so I hope you will take a moment to ponder your own life. You probably will surprise yourself as you remember back to not only the good times but also how you got through the bad times.

Always walk with your Lord knowing that He has been walking with you and carrying you each and every moment of every day.

Go forward and spread the word!

ABOUT THE AUTHOR

I was born, raised and have lived in northern Illinois all of my life except for a short time in southern Wisconsin. I now am semi-retired and live with my wonderful wife of thirty years, Darlene.

I have always wanted to write down my memories so that they could be shared with our family. With the encouragement and support of my wife I actually sat down with paper and pen and began writing thoughts from my childhood. As the pages of notes increased I decided to use the computer to expedite the process. Soon I began to see progress and the development of this book, *"Back When Kids Were Kids."*

I hope you enjoy reading my story and reminiscing about your own early years as much as I did living during those carefree years.

I am a member of the Chicago Writers Association.

22322043R00091

Made in the USA
San Bernardino, CA
04 July 2015